jesus'
love

Jesus' Love
by Premakarini

Paper Street Publishing
Los Angeles, California
www.jesuslovethebook.com

ISBN: 978-0-9825399-0-3
LCC TXu 1-590-682

Book design by Sue Sylvia,
StaircasePressDesign.com

For information on bulk sales discount for schools, non-profits,
corporations and fundraising, please visit www.jesuslovethebook.com.

jesus' love

premakarini

I had always known I was to write *Jesus' love*, but I had no idea just what this experience was to be, no idea how this book was going to affect others.

Immediately I was moved by the way Jesus wrote, the way he immerses the reader in love in a way they haven't experienced before. Every free moment I had I devoted time to *Jesus' love*, often effortlessly for hours, excited to see more of what he had to share. It was impossible to put down, even though I was busy editing on other projects at the time.

Just three weeks later I had *Jesus' love* in a complete manuscript form which I eagerly began to share. The responses were beyond anything I could have expected. Many cried tears of joy and held the book so tenderly just speaking of it. Others read it slowly out loud to me, savoring its wisdom. Everyone loved it and it became apparent it moved them profoundly in a way I have not seen before with a book.

The power of such reactions compelled me to see the larger vision for this book, and I began to appreciate that *Jesus' love* is to reach a wider audience through unlimited distribution and that a large percentage of the profits are to be shared with many charitable organizations, in order to serve as many people globally as possible.
This is the purpose of *Jesus' love*.

So it is with great honor and love that I offer this book. Please feel free to share this with as many loved ones as you are inspired to. You are now a part of this greater vision. Welcome.

With love and gratitude,

Premakarini

I am in no way special
I share this love in the hope that you will join us in it as One
This book belongs to all of us

This is our love

table of *contents*

Preface

You are opening. You demonstrate the power of love; you realize that now is the time.

Welcome home, dear one. Simply trust that the energy of God is behind and in every one of these words, as is the knowing, that you have always known in your heart, and you are being transformed in every moment that you are willing to share these truths, these words of truth. Life is given for this, for this understanding. And you shall realize that this is all there is.

Truth. God. Reality. Love. Life.

It doesn't matter what you call it, it is what is real, what is only real.

Ever yours in love, and endless devotion,
Jesus

This was given to me by Jesus on September 6, 2008, after he shared the section "being God" with me. I realize that these words were given for all of us, so I am deeply honored to be sharing them with you now.
Love and blessings,
Premakarini

Introduction

by premakarini

Inspired by Jesus' teachings, I consider myself to be spiritual, and I follow a wide range of universal enlightened teachings from many sources and religions. If pressed I would say that my religion is Love. I believe in the power of sharing love and improving life for everyone in the world. I believe in our unity, that we are all one in God and love.

When I was in Honduras, serving as a volunteer working in hospice and with the poor, I felt his presence so strongly one day and received a communication in that he wanted me to help him unite everyone and to bring all religions to the truth of his message of love. This is what he came to share, and the true vision that accompanies such love, to see what is real.

It has taken many years to realize exactly what this meant and how it would manifest in my life, but now I realize that sharing my experiences with him and God are to accomplish this in one form, that it will show that experiences of him and the truth are possible, that there are many having and sharing in experiences of him. I am blessed to have beloved friends in my life who share a close, conscious connection with Jesus that is very much as mine is.

He only wants us to know that he is here serving everyone, regardless of our beliefs, or religion, that we are all loved by him, and that he is our brother, that we stand equal to him. I thank you for joining with us now in reading this. It is out of my deepest gratitude to Jesus for being in my life, and all the love and respect I have for him, that I devote myself to bringing his teachings into the world.

I always knew we would write a book one day and I knew that it was to be called simply *Jesus' Love*.
Here it is.

willingness

Willingness is acceptance, trust, humility.

I ask you to be willing, to accept these words with an open heart and mind, to allow the truth to be experienced and known deeply within you.

I ask you to be willing to allow these truths to resonate within you, so that you experience them directly with your being.

When I ask you to be willing I ask you to accept reality with trust, with humility. I am only asking you to trust what is real, to be open to the experience of reality.

The illusion has tricked you so many times it has destroyed your ability to trust. I understand this; I know that you cannot trust.

Be willing to trust these words enough so that you open to the experience of reality and let go of your experience of illusion. Be willing to see illusion for what it is: something that cannot be trusted.

This is the first step in putting your trust in reality.
I am not asking you to trust the illusion.
I am asking you to trust only what is real.

Willingness is the way you open to having the experience of reality.
When you are willing to be open to reality, you experience only what is real.

Only the experience of reality itself will
reveal the truth of these words I share now.
Trust what I say enough in this moment so that you experience reality,
then you will no longer need to trust me, you will know as I know.

I hold open the door to reality so that you may live in reality. This is all.
There is nothing special about me, or anyone else who does this. When you
live in reality you know this, and you will want to be the door to others,
also, you will understand the deep, abiding desire to do so.

I ask you to remove me from the heights
you have placed me upon, from the special place
that you reserve for me, for as you do this,
you stand with me in truth, in reality.

We are equal, you and I, and when you truly experience our
oneness, you assist me more than you realize.

I only ask that you are willing to experience
what is real.

When you are willing, you are honoring
the divine within you. You are placing your trust in God.
I ask you only to trust the divine within you, to place your trust
in God within you.

You can trust God.

trust

I ask you to trust me, to place your trust in what I am sharing with you so that you can experience love.

The trust I ask of you is for you, so you can have the wisdom of this experience and can let go of everything else that is not love.

As long as you hold onto your fears, doubts —even expectations— all these hold you out of the experience of love I am sharing with you now.

For whatever you experience, you experience through fear, through doubt and you do not have the pure, full experience of love that transforms you.

This love waits for you to come into the full experience of it. It is the most powerful experience that you can have.

Most of you have not experienced real love; most of you have only experienced a small fraction of this love.

You have an idea about trust. You think trust is a lack of suspicion.

Trust is when there is no doubt.

As long as you doubt these words, as long as you hold doubt about what I am saying here, you are not giving your trust to me.

You live in doubt to varying degrees, far more than you live in trust, which is why you have only experienced a mere glimpse of the love there is to experience.

You live in fear, always trying to protect yourself from someone or something.
Until you are aware that this is how you live, you cannot let all this go.

Look at all the doubts you have had in just the past day or week and you will know in your heart how you are holding yourself out of my love.

Even in this moment you doubt what I am saying here, it is hard for you to take these words into your heart, yet this is what I am asking you to do.

"But I don't believe fully in you," you may say.
This may be so, but what about love?

Are you willing to experience this love? Are you willing to be humble and at least consider what I am sharing with you?

I do not ask you to believe in me. I do not ask you to believe in love, or what I share. I ask you to allow the experience of love into your life, so you know this love is real. Then you know that I am real. You experience me, when you experience love.

I can only show you how you can do this.

You can experience love fully when you let go of all your fears and doubts.

I do not want you to think you are love.
I want you to **know** that you are love.

You do not need another's love to experience love.
Trust this.

When you trust this, you never experience fear with anyone
again and you never doubt anyone's love again.

You may recognize it in a more limited form, or expression, but
you also recognize they hold back the experience of love that
is possible between you both simply out of fear, and you love
them without needing their love.

There is no evidence or proof of love because there is no need
for evidence when something is real.

Love is its own reality.
<u>*Love is reality.*</u>

Love cannot be found in illusion, in fear, doubt and mistrust.

Do you see how these create illusion?

Of what is illusion made?
Fear, doubt, confusion, mistrust, pain and suffering.

Love exists beyond illusion and is always real.

This is why if you bring your fears and doubts into your heart
they dissolve immediately.
Illusion cannot exist in reality.

I offer this experience of love for you now. I humbly ask that you open your heart and allow this experience into your life and into the lives of your loved ones. Help them to experience this love through your love for them. I humbly ask you to trust that this love is real and to put aside all your fears and doubts that keep you separate from this profound experience of love. You will know when you have let them go, it will not be possible for you to fear or doubt again, once this love is fully experienced. For then shall your heart be open, and love is all you will know.

You are even afraid to have such a transformation, for you know that you will never be the same again. Put away your fear. It is not even real. Give your fear to me; let me hold it for you, so that you may know love.

I humbly ask you to be willing to have this experience.
This is my love.
This is your love.
This is our love.
I am with you always in this love; remember this,
Jesus

forgiveness

---

*Forgiveness is to give your self true vision,
to see what is real.*

*When you see what is real, that love is only what is real,
you see that there is nothing to forgive, that all you have to forgive
is merely illusion.*

*The world that you live in, that you believe is real, the events in
your life that you feel have hurt you or have given you the
idea, even, that you in some way need to forgive, are not real.
They are merely your dream of reality, a dream that you are to
awaken from as soon as you realize the truth of this.*

*So you see, there is nothing to forgive except for your own
illusion that there is a need to forgive anything that has
happened in your life.*

*When you understand this, healing occurs
and your vision of reality is restored.*

*There is nothing else for you to do except realize that love is
the only thing that is real, that reality is love and that you are
love. You extend love to all when you realize this and share this
with everyone.*

*You are here to help awaken everyone else to this truth, so
that you stand in the true reality of love and live in this reality,
sharing it with everyone. This is all that has to happen for you
to awaken.*

*Once you awaken you help others to awaken because now they
stand where you stand and see what you see and they love life
as you do.*

*This is what I came to do, and still do here in the
world. When you join with me in this you stand
where I do. I am always with you, waiting for you
to realize this. All you have to do is awaken,
to open your eyes to this truth.*

*This is the greatest gift you can share with your loved ones, with the world,
for this is what we came here to do. And awakening happens in a moment,
an instant. It can be as simple as sharing a smile, or holding the vision for a
loved one when they are struggling in their illusion. It can be as simple as
reminding your brother that he is getting caught in the illusion, that he has
stepped out of reality for an instant and all he need do is to remember this
and return.*

*This is all I am here to do in this moment:
to remind you of the truth.*

Forgiveness is remembering.
*You forget that love is the only reality and you try to get what you can
out of the illusion that you are in.*
This is forgetting.
Instead of giving your Self the truth by remembering what is real.

*You forget that illusion cannot give you anything;
it always seems to be offering you something.
You crave reality, and you have got caught up in
looking everywhere in the illusion for what is real,*

*all the time forgetting that it cannot give you
what is real, for it is not real itself.*

*Only what is real can give you what is real.
Only reality can give you what is real.*
Life is often veiled by the illusion, this dream of life, which is merely a
shadow of what is real. Your great thinker Plato taught of this in his famous
simile of the caves, where everyone mistook the shadows for reality, and
when they stepped into the light, out of the cave of their perception, they
saw the truth.

Forgiveness is seeing what is real. Forgiveness is having true
vision and sharing this vision with others. There is no need to struggle to
forgive another when you see reality for what it is. You realize that everyone
makes mistakes because they cannot realize what is real, and they live out
of an illusion, they act from this idea and this is the only reason anyone
suffers in the world.
Suffering keeps you in the world of illusion.

It is not possible to suffer in the reality of love.

*Forgiveness is giving your self this reality;
forgiveness is giving this reality to the world.*

*Forgiveness leads to freedom. True freedom
is when you realize that love is the only reality.*

Then you are free from all suffering, from your past, for all that you have
thought was real is but illusion.

I taught forgiveness so you give yourself this freedom, and in giving yourself
this freedom, you give this to everyone. In this way you see forgiveness in its
true light, that it gives you freedom from all you do not wish to experience in
life. I did not mean for you to suffer more in attempting to forgive something
in your life that brought you deep pain. This misperception has only led to
more suffering, which is not forgiveness at all.

9

So many of you struggle with forgiveness only because you do not understand what these words mean. Now you are clear.
You stand with me in this moment. I am with you, holding this vision for you. I love you with a love that overflows from my heart, filling your own. When you understand how I love you, you will understand that there is no need for you to even ask me to forgive you.

You need never ask me for forgiveness, for there is nothing to be forgiven, in reality.

Only illusion insists on the need for forgiveness, and demands it from another, for only illusion imagines that it is possible to be hurt, or attacked.
There is no need for forgiveness in reality, only in illusion.

I do not want your guilt, I only ask for your love.
Leave your guilt behind with all that is illusion. Then you are free from all suffering, from your past, for all the suffering that you have thought was real is but part of the world of illusion.

Stand with me in the utter freedom and love of reality. You are free, now. When you know this, you are with me, always.
I am your brother,
Jesus

freedom

Freedom is the ability to live in reality.
Freedom is the ability to experience what is real.

When you are free you live in love, in reality. Freedom releases you from all pain, fear, suffering, and guilt, from all that is not real. Everything that is not real imprisons you in a world of illusion. You cannot see the walls of this prison, yet they veil the truth of what is real, holding you in a world where you cannot escape until you see it for what it is – pure illusion.

Your beliefs, your fears, your guilt all create this world and keep you caught in your self-made prison.

Freedom is releasing your self from the illusion, you do this by forgiving yourself for making this illusory world in the first place, letting it fall away from your perception, being replaced by love, the only thing that is real.
When you release all that is not real, you are then free to experience all the love that overflows from your heart. This love is always in your heart, but you are not able to experience it because you are stuck in fear, guilt and pain.

Freedom is the experience of love and only love.

Loving yourself truly is simply allowing the experience of love within you, and letting this love radiate to everyone.

When you love your self truly you free yourself. This is why I teach only love. For love is all that is real and is your true being. There is no thing else that is real. Love liberates you from all your ideas, thinking and perception about what is real, it allows you to see with love, and through love.

This is important – seeing <u>with</u> love and <u>through</u> love. You are still trying to see through the body; through your two physical eyes, which are only capable of such limited perception, and are so prone to distort reality because all they do is transfer an image of what you think you see at any given time.

If you knew how fear prevents you from seeing so much, how it distorts everything you look at and try to perceive, you would see what I see, you would only see what is real.

No one teaches you true vision, to see with love. Yet this is the only way to see anything. See the world now with me, with my love and through my love in this instant. Such an instant is the holy instant, which is expressed in "A Course In Miracles" and my other books, which I have shared with you.

I am here now to share my vision with you, to have you see with love so that you are free.

I said that the truth will set you free, and this is what I meant. I also said I am the truth, the way, the light. When I say this I mean it, for I am experiencing the vision through love at this time. I see the world as it really is, as love.

I see you as love, as the truth and the way and the light, also. This is the vision I want to share with you, I want you to see who you truly are, that you are one with me, always, whether you are aware of this or not. I share this with you now, humbly, asking you to accept this vision, to share this vision with me now.

Acceptance is love in action.

*Acceptance is continually letting go with love. See everything
as an opportunity for growth through acceptance.
Gently embrace everything in your life with love and acceptance.
This is how awareness grows, through acceptance.*

When you love, you have true awareness, through acceptance.

*I love life in a way that you have yet to experience, and it is this experience
I intend for you through this book. This book shares with you not only this
vision through love, but it connects you to me, so you can experience what I
experience. In this way you are free, right now, in this moment. Can you
feel it dear one? Imagine my joy that you are here with me now, letting this
freedom release you from all your fears, all your prisons of doubt,
confusion and of lack.*

You are free with me forever. It only takes a moment to awaken to this truth, to experience this much love. This is your freedom.

*I love you with a love that is so pure, so free, and you experience this right
now in your heart. Simply feel the love expand in your heart and I am here
with you now, loving you. Put aside all other thoughts or ideas about whether
you deserve such an experience of love. Give me now your doubts that you
can have this experience of love. All I ask is for you to receive this love, now in
this moment, and to remember in each moment that I am with you, that
I share love with you, so that you can experience the love that you are.*

*If you can do this for me in this moment, please accept also my deepest
gratitude to you. I am so deeply thankful for you giving me this moment.
Feel with me the immense joy and bliss that I experience in this moment in
sharing who I am with you, the love that I am, that you are! I am with you
in every moment, now and always.*

*I am simply your brother,
Jesus*

holy instant

---

*Be willing to recognize and see God everywhere,
in every moment.
Miracles are happening all the time, all
around you.
You just have to be willing to be aware of this.
This is resting in God. This is trusting in God.
Rest in God's being. You can do this all the
time – it is simply a choice.*

Trust each moment as an opportunity to experience your being.

Welcome each moment for what it brings uniquely to your experience. Each moment is very different; allow each difference gently into your experience. You are not any experience; you are so much more.

You are divine.

Know that what you experience does not, cannot define you. Understand this. It is just an experience; let it pass through you. Be transparent, nothing needs to enter your life, nothing needs to be you unless you claim it to be so. Each experience that comes to you comes for a particular reason. Each experience is an opportunity to go deeper into your being.

Recognize your divinity in each moment.
Each moment is an opportunity to go deeper into your divine being.
As you become intimate with your own divine being, you open the door to
being truly present. The greatest gift you can share with another being is to
recognize and be present to the divinity within them.
This is really being with another.

This is the only time you can really share with
another that is real.

This is a holy instant.

Share from your being.
You simply allow the sharing to happen as an extension of your being.
Let the sharing happen, naturally, from your innermost being, trusting that
each moment is perfect.

Realize the divine being you are and simply be this.
In all your most enlightened moments this is your
experience.

Establish your identity in the divine.
Do not identify with your experiences, your emotions, thoughts, ideas – these
are not you. Live your divinity, allow the divine to experience through you,
share your divinity with the world.
This is who you are.

Gently share this with everyone, with patience and kindness.
This is respecting the divine being in everyone. And it is what will fulfill
you the most in this life, whether you are aware of this yet, or not.
You will come to this realization at some point in your existence.

I merely place it gently in your awareness, in your mind now,
in this moment. What you do with this truth is up to you.
But know that it is like a seed, and one day will mature in you, and you
can nurture this growth now, or wait, but this is your opportunity now.

Each moment that you rest in God is a holy instant.

You are eternal. Each moment you experience this is a holy instant. Each moment is given to you so you may experience the truth. Time is only here so you may experience love. Time is not what you think it is. When you allow the truth of time to penetrate your being you will awaken into timelessness. I am here in this moment sharing this holy instant with you. Simply be with me and be willing to experience this one holy instant; allow these words to penetrate your being.

You experience a holy instant when you remember that this world is but a dream. This is all time is for: to give you but one moment to awaken, to realize this. This is all it takes.

Every moment is an opportunity to share and experience love.

All you have to be is willing to allow the experience of a holy instant to transform you. There are an infinite number of opportunities for this to happen, it is up to you to be open and willing for the experience to change you.

It is as simple as changing your mind about what is real. For this to happen it only takes one moment of reality.

Each holy instant is a window into eternity; a moment when you experience only what is real.

Every moment we share love, receive love, give love, acknowledge love and realize we are love; the moment itself expands through love to all eternity, to infinity...
You experience the eternal now.

Only the experiences of love that you experience in life are real. The moments you share love, give love and experience love are only real. Everything else is illusion and need not be accepted, or understood. You waste time trying to comprehend and come to terms with what is illusion, when it is not necessary.

When you awaken you realize that all of your efforts in time were to realize the love that is possible in this holy instant.

It is only your belief in the illusion that makes it real, that gives it any power at all.

Every instant that you are free from thought or misperception you experience a holy instant.

Each holy instant is a taste of eternity, a way to remain in reality. When you allow yourself to experience what is real, you are no longer in the illusion.

Each holy instant is a moment you experience timelessness, the bliss and joy that is unending, that is eternally yours, waiting for you to come into realization that this is really all there ever is.

When you experience a holy instant you are present, you are present to reality.
This is what presence is: you are fully in reality.

A holy instant allows you to experience your sacred presence.

When you step into eternity you experience your divinity.
Be with me in this moment and experience your divinity, your sacred presence with me now.

You feel you still need visible evidence. But you cannot trust this illusion over what is real. Do you see this? You are still giving way too much power to illusion, allowing it to govern your beliefs still. Let go of illusion, let go of

needing evidence, or proof, this is only more illusion. You are looking for more illusion within the illusion…this will continue until you choose reality and let go of illusion.
This is trust in action.

See how easy it is to live this way?
It is a simple choice, a simple way of being.

See with the deep gratitude and humility of divine being. How gentle this perception, how grateful, how loving it is! How humble! Be ever touched and graced by this energy that is being freely bestowed upon you from your divine presence infinitely.

When you live from this divine being, you live as God. You are full of divine energy, presence and awareness. Your whole being is God.

Be in the presence of this love without question and with simple gratitude and gentle acceptance. Move more deeply into this love with grace, with the understanding that this is nurturing yourself; this is deeply serving yourself so you may serve others better.
You are always of service. Do not discriminate with your time. It is not real. It is just a measure of experience here, a way to measure your experiences in your life. Do you see how you are now moved to share this more and more with others, and how you are deepening your experience of God the more that you do this?

I am with you in every moment, now and always, as your brother Jesus.

God

You have never left God.
You can awaken to this reality right now. As soon as
you awaken to this truth, you are in reality.

You have only left God in your mind. You have made this whole dream,
this entire illusion from this one idea that you are separate from God.
It is not possible, even for you to be separate from God, for this would be
saying you are somehow without yourself. Only an illusion, or an illusory
belief would suggest separation.

When I say God is within you, that Christ is within
you, I am saying that you are God; you are Christ.

When you realize that the very illusion that supposes you are separate from
God completely depends on such an idea in the first place, you will awaken
to the truth that God is always with you.

You can experience God any time you want.
You can experience God in your heart this very
instant simply by turning within.
It only takes one instant to do this.

You see, you have been looking outside of yourself for God. This is how you made this illusory dream world – by looking for God outside of yourself, by forgetting to look within you. You needed a place to look so you made an illusory world outside of yourself to look for yourself in, to look for God. It's okay, you have only forgotten. All you have to do is remember to awaken, and turn inward.

This is why I say the kingdom of heaven is within you.
It hasn't gone anywhere in all eternity, it is always there, it is you who goes away, by forgetting it is there. You simply forgot the more you looked outside. Now remember and experience the love in your heart.

Do you see how easy it is to awaken?

You are not asked to believe that you are God. It is not a question of faith; you are here to experience it, right now in this moment.

I am here right now asking you to experience this with me; will you join me in this experience? Do not worry about having any particular experience of this through your body, or senses, simply know in this moment that this is happening, and allow this to unfold. Allow God within you to reveal the love within you.

The more you look within and experience the love that is in your heart, that is God's presence within you, the stronger your experience of love is and you know you are God.

Do not put off till tomorrow what can be experienced here and now: give yourself this one holy instant now to experience that you are God. I am here with you right now, holding open this experience for you. Feel the love overflowing from your heart in glad recognition of this one eternal truth. All you have to do is be open to receive this experience. It has waited for you for all eternity.

If you knew how much you are helping me to serve the world by receiving this love, by opening to this experience, you would not hesitate for one moment. This is all I ask of you: allow yourself to experience my love in this moment. Be willing to feel the love that I am, that you are.

This is what you came here to experience: love

Let go of everything else. Whatever else pulls on you to be experienced, let it go. Go beyond your mind, your thoughts; simply rest in the love.
The deeper your experience of love, the more you allow yourself to live in love, and with love, the more you awaken to who you are: God.

This is all it takes.
Enough love.

love

Only love is real.
There is only love; the only real experience is love.

Everything is created from love so when you
rest in love you are creating with love.

Love is all I experience so I invite you to experience only love with me now.

When you choose love, and only love in every
moment, in every situation, until you realize the
truth that love is only what is real and that there is
only love and only ever will be.

When you live in love, all that is not love simply dissolves into love. Every
fear dissolves in this love, so peacefully and beautifully that you will wonder
how you ever imagined that any of your fears could have been real.

For the love in you will be so strong no fear
will be able to remain in its presence.

Fear may rise within you, and you may notice it, but then you will see it simply dissolve and you won't even feel it. Your body will still be calm, you will experience that deep, all pervading sense of peace and calm that is continuously present in you: you will be undisturbed.

This is the experience of love in you.

Then you simply know you are love for you feel it throughout your whole being. You feel invincible, unshakable, for you will be.
And your love continues to grow in strength and power. For your love is infinitely strong and powerful, by its very nature, you just haven't experienced this fully yet.

You will look back at the times you used to shake in fear and smile at how you used to be, like the antics of a small child.
And you will experience the peace of knowing. You need never return to living in fear ever again, you are so at peace it seems to you to be impossible.

And bliss, the bliss of knowing will pervade this deep sense of peace as you realize this peace, this love, that this bliss is who you are and life is simply for you to experience this truth.

Your life is for you to share this sacred truth with everyone.

You will know this so deeply inside of you that you will never doubt again. Doubt may arise, but it will simply fade and dissolve in this deep knowing that you are love.

When you live perpetually in love, you begin to realize that love is the source of all your strength, all your power.

You will realize that this is the only strength upon which you can truly depend.

This strength grows the more you depend on it. It is pure power. It is the only power. Once you realize what power really is, you will only choose love. Many look for power outside of themselves. To the extent that you do this, you have forgotten that real power is only love.

Love brings you all the experiences that you need in life.

When you experience the power of love you begin to tap into infinite power, truth and wisdom. There is unlimited power inside you. All you have to do is to be aware that it is all within you. Experience this now: reach deep into your heart, feel the presence of power here. Let yourself be immersed totally in this experience. Do not be afraid of your own power.

Experience your infinity: love.

Love is an infinite experience. Love is the ultimate experience; love is what has the most value. When you value love, you have the experience of true value.

What has value comes from love and shares love.

You are here to give the recognition that you are love to all your loved ones. This is the greatest gift you can give to another being: to gently remind them that they are love, that they do not need love, because they are radiant love and that they need never beg another for their love or ask for love from another out of a feeling, a misperception of needing love.

You are all here to be love, not to be loved. You do not need to be loved; you are so beloved. The love that you are is infinite, where is your need for love?

See, I am here to remind you that you are love; you do not need to look outside of who you are for love. Many of you believe that you lack love, that somehow you need to be loved so that you can experience love. This is where all conflict comes from in your relationships. You hold expectations about how you need to be loved, how you want to be loved, all the time forgetting that you are love.

You even attack another if you feel they are withholding love in some way from you. Can you see how this only comes from your misperceptions about love?

Let yourself experience the love that you are in this moment.

All it takes is one moment of pure willingness. Put aside all of your ideas about love. Allow my love for you to open you to your love. Put aside all your ideas about not being worthy. There is nothing you have done that would cause me to not share love with you. Know that anything that you have done that has caused you any guilt is only in illusion, not in reality.

I ask you to do this for me and for everyone. For as you awaken, you help others to awaken. This is what we are here for. We are brothers and sisters; we are all one in love. There are no exceptions to this; there are none who are less worthy of the experience of their love, indeed, those who feel this way need the awareness of their love more than ever.

I ask you as your brother to help with this, for this is how we serve the world. Know that as you help another to awaken to the love that they are, you experience all the love that you are.

I say this for all those who do not consider themselves ready perhaps to join me in this service. You are ready now. I am with you; you are not alone in this. The more you are with me consciously; the more you will realize I was always with you, and I will always be with you, as we are all with each other.

Thank you for sharing me so directly and for letting me be in your world in this moment. It is a great honor to serve with you, always.

I am with you in love,
Jesus

I am the way

I said that I am the way because only love is real; everything else is illusion.
You hear these words and imagine that I am speaking of the personality's way, but this is not what I mean, or that my way is the only way and everyone else's way is wrong.

There is only one way, only one reality and that is love.
This has nothing to do with the personality.
The personality is made from illusion.
The personality's highest purpose is to express love.

Over the years since I shared my teaching I have longed to clarify many of the teachings that survive today.
I have done this through many of you and I will continue to do so.
The written word is easily misunderstood by the mind. When I spoke these words originally I was able to present the teaching clearly before all minds and to respond to any confusions or doubts.

Those in my presence were able to experience my love and did not need the words to know the teachings are real; the words were used merely to clear all doubts and confusion from the minds, to reinforce the direct experience I was able to give.
This is what I give to you now.

Read these words, but feel my presence, my love behind them. Do not merely take the words inside you, take my love, experience my love inside of you. Let this love fill you in this moment. I am here with you, taking your hand sharing this love with you in this moment, wherever you are, whatever you have done, whoever you are.
Nothing else matters.

Only the entire experience of love will reveal the truth of these words I share now.

I ask you to do this for me. Help me by doing this. Help your loved ones to do this, with me yes, but also with you. This love I give to you I ask you to take this so you have it to share with others. Know the more you share this love, the more I can pour into your heart so it is overflowing.

Know this: if you do not feel this love, it is only because you are forgetting to share it with everyone, because you have forgotten how love feels.

You experience love as pure bliss, pure joy, pure peace.

This is why I say,
"love everyone, especially those who you think are your enemies."
So you are filled to overflowing with love.
So you live in love.

Premakarini is our beloved sister; we are all one family. Premakarini is so overflowing with love that in my presence, or in the presence of deeply shared love, tears flow. These tears are of pure love, of pure devotion and surrender, of the immense joy she feels with the experience of love. This is why she is known as Premakarini, which means overflowing with love. "Prema" is love in Sanskrit, "karini" means overflowing, radiating love.

This is why she honors this sacred name. It is a remembrance of her gift of sharing love, of her purpose. This is how she experiences the divine within. The more she loves, the more enlightened she is, and the more love she has to share with the world.

Love is infinite, eternal, everflowing.

I am simply here to remind you that you are this love, it is within you — it will flow, pour from you like an eternal fountain, the more you share love with others.

I share love with you to remind you of this. You only need to share the love that you are at all times, in every moment, with everyone, no exceptions.

I ask this of you. Make no exceptions. I extend this to you, I make no exceptions and I only humbly request you do the same.

Love belongs to everyone. It is the birthright of everyone on earth. Do not exclude any one from the love that flows from within you, as it is God's love.

I ask this because as you exclude another from the experience of this love, you exclude yourself. For you cannot hold back the love from only one person, it is held back from your experience as soon as you do this. I do not want you to ever be without this love.

Naturally, your ego will object, but you are not your ego, or your mind, and as the love that you are simply acknowledge this truth and simply love your ego and mind even though they object.

Love everyone.
This is all I came to teach. This is all I ask of you. This is all you ever need do.

love your enemy

When I said love your greatest enemy it was because this is the easiest way to experience the truth of love.

When you love even in the face of adversity, criticism and judgment, and the trials you face with others, you know that nothing can take away from the love that you are, or from the experience of love, once you realize this.

Love is such a powerful force; it is the only thing that is real.
Fear, anger, mistrust – none of these can change or take away from love in any way.
Love stands supreme.

When you realize the power of love and you stand in this power, you realize you are invincible.
This is the power you seek, the safety you crave.
Love and only love assures you of this.

Love is the greatest and only power there is.

Let all that is not love fall away from your experience. Simply drop it.
You do not have to give it any attention, even.
Put your attention only on what is real in any situation: love.
Then you experience reality simply and purely as it is: love.

*Allowing yourself to experience reality is
loving yourself, respecting yourself.*

*You disrespect yourself by holding yourself in fear. How can this be loving
to yourself or others?*

*You continually disrespect yourself by not allowing yourself to
simply be in reality.*
You postpone the experience purely out of fear or guilt –
*thinking it is not for you because of _____ and you fill this in with some
fear or guilt – something usually in your past which you think cannot be
changed, which convinces you that you do not deserve to experience love,
something that is not even real.*

This is not loving, respectful or kind.
This is giving power ultimately to illusion.
You disrespect yourself by putting the illusion above and before yourself.

*Simply the fact you think you have an enemy
means you have fallen into illusion.*

*When this happens it is a reminder to wake up and return to reality, your
"enemy" is giving you an opportunity to awaken, and to experience more
love than you could possibly imagine. Of course, this requires some humility
and trust, at first, but once you realize that there is no enemy, but only
another soul who would help you awaken, then you are free to respond
with love.*

*Only the love between us is real and everything else
is pure illusion and that by just realizing this you
enter Reality.*

*This is all there really is, but out of fear you make other "realities" up as
you go along. These "realities" are never real. Fear only makes the illusion
appear real.*

When you have a true vision of reality, it is because it is always real, and close, and it is always waiting for you to realize it.

Love always waits to be realized.

Love comes from your deepest, innermost being; love never comes from outside of you. When you love your enemies you know you are love, you directly experience what love really is. I am here guiding you, loving through you, even in the moments you find it hardest to be loving. This is my promise to you.

When you recognize your brother in the face of hostility, in the face of conflict, I am with you completely.

You are never alone, and when you love in the most challenging of occasions, I am with you, by your side, urging you to reach even deeper into your heart, for both of you stand with me, always, and I know that this is such an opportunity for you both to awaken, and this is all I want for you both.

Remember that as you awaken by remembering to love, you awaken your brother who you imagine to be your enemy in that moment, also.

Sometimes you are so stubborn, so closed, it takes a challenging, even life threatening event to awaken you, and it takes a brother who loves you deeply to act as an enemy to be the one to wake you. Simply remember this in your heart when you are feeling unfairly attacked, see that it takes deep, great love to choose to be an enemy in this situation, and this will humbly remind you of the love you both share.

I am proud of you, ever your brother, Jesus.

sharing love

Love is the way we awaken.
We awaken by sharing love with each other.
All sharing is a way to communicate love, to express love
between two beings.

The most important thing in life is to share love.
Love is only realized when it is shared. Love is an active expression.
Love is more than being loving yourself; love is allowing love in from others
through allowing them to be loving in your presence.

When you allow another being to be loving in your
presence, you allow him to be all that he is.

The more you express love, the more love you share, the more you are being
yourself.

If another person's love makes you uncomfortable in any way, makes you
question their motives, or your motives, recognize this: you are not allowing
the full expression of your love.

For if you cannot allow the full expression of who you are, then you cannot
allow others to share love fully, also.

In the world, love is not allowed to be openly expressed, out of fear of miscommunication, or misunderstanding, of giving the wrong idea to another being. Only this idea itself is the only error you can make!

Sharing love is the ultimate expression of self. The more love you share, the more fulfilled you are.

The more you share love the more you remove the belief in the lack of love. The more love you share, the more you realize that love is abundant, ever present and unlimited. Sharing love frees you from all experience of limitation. When others experience your love, you remind them of their unlimited love and potential.

Sharing transforms illusion into reality.

The illusion depends on ideas and beliefs of limitation, lack, and scarcity. When you share you give power to reality, and you weaken illusion. If everyone shared everything all the time, there would only be abundance. So many look for the experience of abundance without thinking of sharing, this is the missing element in all the teachings that you are following about creating abundance.

Once you understand that creating reality depends on ideas that belong to reality, you will share continually with everyone, with no exceptions. Sharing not only creates reality, it transforms illusion into reality. Sharing love is the most empowering act you can do.

You experience love because you are love.

Share without hope or expectation that others will share with you in the same way you have done so.
When you share with others, so often you fear they will not reciprocate, that they will take advantage of your kindness and generosity. Give freely in the trust and certainty that they are just as sharing as you are, no matter how they act. For in reality, they are.

And I tell you, in truth, it is far better to be taken advantage of, than to withhold your sharing.

For when you share, you share reality. When you withhold sharing you share illusion. Always choose to live in reality, no matter what.

I tell you this: You can never be taken advantage of in reality. You can only be taken advantage of in illusion. Indeed, illusion itself continually takes advantage of you by controlling your perception and keeping you captive in its prison.

This, I hope shares some light on why I said turn the other cheek: if someone strikes you, offer the other cheek. In so doing you are showing them that they cannot harm you in reality. This was what I intended to teach by saying this.

If someone approaches you in great fear, offer only the love of reality. This is all you can ever truly share with another being; there is nothing else. If you respond in fear, in defense, you miss the opportunity to reassure your brother that only reality; only love is real. And you are taken out of reality the moment you choose to share the illusion of fear with them. You have to ask yourself is anything worth this?

Always choose to remain in reality, no matter what you experience. Always remember that you are choosing to live in illusion the moment this fear of being taken advantage of crosses your mind. Allow your self to let go more and give love and affection to everyone without concern. Trust me in this, even if you cannot trust them, or their actions.

When you truly love another being, the love you share is sacred.

You project illusion out of fear in your relationships; rarely are you ever simply with someone as they are. This is why you are to only share love.

But in relationship both can be hurt, both are required to trust each other, otherwise no true sharing can take place.

Think of this before you choose to be in fear alone.

When you share love, you are both experiencing the fear of loss of this love. Your loved one is just as afraid as you are. The more love you both share, your beloved sees more of you, of your love, so that now he or she has more to lose, much more. But all of this is illusion. And you can see their illusion, just as they can see yours.

Do you see how fear separates you? It prevents you from sharing what is real in every opportunity for sharing. And fear can be so strong that even when the love is shared, is spoken of, it is not believed.

So be gentle with each other. Be kind. You are never alone in fear. Simply remember fear is not real and help each other to remember this always.

Allow yourself to go beyond the experience of love that you have experienced so far in life.

Allow real love to happen between you both, allow yourself to share love in its purest form. Allow yourself the full experience of love. Live this love at a deeper level; choose to remain in this love. When you live this love, you experience how it is purer, stronger. This happens when you share only love.

Fear contaminates, dilutes the love that can be shared.

Fear separates you; it weakens you. Fear wants you to feel alone, to feel like only you are capable of being hurt in any situation. This is where this feeling of fear is really coming from. This place: illusion.

Only illusion causes you to experience fear. This is what illusion does, and how it sustains and perpetuates itself.
I invite you to drop this illusion, to drop this fear and rest in the love between you. Remember to be certain. With certainty comes reality.

Only recognize what is real between you.

*When you perceive fear between you and another, it is because
you are projecting fear onto them and between you.
This is only sharing fear, and you are missing the chance to experience the
love between you when you allow fear into your shared experience.*

*You want your relationships to last, to endure and to be real. Relationships
can only exist in love and through love.
When you are hurting emotionally and you feel deep pain, this is when you
need love and need to love the most, and yet you close your heart trying to
protect it in some way.*

*If a relationship changes form, it doesn't mean the love is gone,
or that you can no longer love this being.
Realize that it really is an opportunity to love even more.*

*There is some fear – fear of separation, of loss, but you face this fear and
love them anyway.*

You take the love between you to a higher, deeper place. This is how love grows, every time you face fear you transform it into love and the love naturally grows.

The more love grows, the less fear you experience.

You realize that there is nothing to fear.
There is nothing to fear and everything to love.

*Fear is just when you are having trouble remembering love.
Your life is for you to remember who you are, which is love.
Do not waste your life in fear; this is not the purpose of your life.
All it takes is one experience of love.*

The greatest gift you can give to both yourself and your loved one is love that exists regardless of what

form it takes. When you allow the love between you to grow into its most unconditional form, relationships take care of themselves.

You do not have to concern yourself with what form love is to take. Love will take the form it is most served by, bringing you only bliss.
This is the love you seek in relationship.

When we share love we are reminded that we are all love, that love is all there is between us.

When you are too busy sharing love, you cease to look for love.
You experience yourself as love, and as you allow this experience to deepen, you live in awe of the power of your love, and you realize that you can do anything with enough love.

Sharing love can happen in the smallest of exchanges, a smile, opening the door for someone, taking the time to talk to someone and share some encouragement, listening with kindness. When your intention is to share love, you will know exactly what is needed in every moment.

The more you share love, the more your heart opens and you see the world very differently, you notice when others are in need, you understand when to act and how to share with others. It takes a shift of perception of being willing to remain in the heart, of keeping the heart open to others.

The healing that you experience is so transformational when this happens; your whole life is changed.
You live in a state of perpetual grace.

Everything you need comes to you naturally; you live in bliss.
You radiate this bliss and love to everyone in your presence, and it uplifts the world. This is what you are here to do. You may think your life is for other reasons, you may think that your life is only for the purposes you are already living. But the greatest purpose you are here to live is to share love.

Many of you hold back out of fear. Fear is just confessing that you think the illusion may be real. No matter how much fear you experience, remember this does not mean it is real. Do not allow fear's presence to suggest its "reality."

It's okay to experience fear, as long as you do not allow the experience of fear to hold you back. It is at this time, more than ever, that you need to share love to dissolve the fear.

Any experience of fear is, and always will be, an illusion.

If you share fear instead of love, you take others deeper into illusion; whereas when you share love, you free yourself and others from illusion.

When you share, you extend yourself through love and you experience just how infinite, how abundant you are. The more you share, the more you have to share.

This is how abundance is always experienced; there is no other way. Abundance is our recognition of the power of sharing with each other, a celebration of our oneness.

Sharing is really just recognizing that we are all one. That we are all love.

Jesus
Thank you for sharing me in your world.

being God

Sharing is how God lives upon the earth.

Sharing is the only real way to live and to experience life.
Sharing is the way to experience your divinity.

*You are God. When you share as God does you know
this, you experience this. This is why you are here.*

Sharing is the ultimate expression of communicating; sharing is
the ultimate experience of connection.

We experience our oneness when we share with others. There is no limit to
how much we share; we are infinite. When we give everything we are to
others, we experience everything for ourselves.

Sharing is the way to experience your being.
Share from your being.
Simply allow the sharing to happen as an extension of your
being. Let the sharing happen, naturally, from your innermost
being, trusting that each moment is perfect.

When you share, you give of yourself.

You are so much more than you think you are.
The more you share of yourself, of your love, the more others will be
reached and deeply moved to the core of their being. Such sharing is
transformational, both for you and they.

Sharing is how you know you are God, because God is always sharing with everyone.

God is always sharing love with us, it's up to us how much we experience.
The more love we share, the more love comes through us, and the more love
we experience in life.

The more you share love the more you experience God.

God is always waiting for us to share with others. We only choose not to share
out of fear, lack or some limitation that we perceive. When we don't share we
are stuck in illusion. Sharing is the way out of illusion. Sharing is the way to
experience reality, and to share the experience of reality with others.

Sharing is giving of God, of experiencing God.
The more we share the more we realize God on earth.

Sharing is the way God's will is experienced.

When you live love and live your divinity you honor the divine in all life.
You honor God by identifying with God.
You deny God by denying that you are God.
You are asked to step into your divinity in every moment, to live your divinity.

Do not wait for this to happen to you; do not wait for an experience of the
Divine for this to begin.

Your life as God begins now in this moment.

There is no reason for you to not experience the Divine in everything, in every moment. Simply the fact that you are not means you are refusing to have this experience for some reason. It is up to you to figure out what you are waiting for.

Are you waiting for some magical out of this world experience to transform you? Are you waiting for a revelation, a certain kind of miracle? Are you waiting for divine powers such as I demonstrated? You do not need to walk on water to be God. You are God, now.

You can do more than walk on water; I want you to dance on the water with me.
This is the vision I hold for you, will you share it with me now? This is how powerful you are, this is but one of the many things that you can do.
You can do anything, if you but knew.

If you are waiting for anything, it just means you do not trust that you are God. You are still in doubt. Simply recognize this doubt as part of the illusion, as not real, and move into the truth that you are God. See yourself as God. This is being God; this is resting in God. This is all you are asked to do.

See the divine in everyone and know that you are God and invite everyone into this presence.

You look outside for a demonstration. You wait for an invitation from the Divine in another being, when you are the demonstration itself, simply waiting to be.
You don't even have to do anything. You are simply asked to be God.
In being God you radiate the divine presence and this in itself awakens everyone with you. Trust in this. This is what is real.

Look not to your brother to see God within another, to experience God, but look to yourself. Look within yourself; see the Christ, the Divine within you and share this with your brother and sister and you will experience God for both of you.

Now your loved one has the opportunity to join with you in God.

Be humble; be gentle and patient and kind. If your brother refuses to be God with you, continue to extend the invitation, without fear or judgment, through your demonstration. Know that you have stood where he now stands and allow the Divine through you to reach him.
He is calling out for this invitation more than ever at this time. Answer his call with your love and gentle patience.

Whether he is willing or not in the moment you share with him does not matter, for there will come a time when he will know, when he will awaken to the gentle truth you have extended to him and it will happen because the seed of recognition you have planted in his awareness has grown into realization in him.

Your sharing, your willingness to join with him in God is then fully received. You plant the seed of Truth in your willingness to share God with him.

Do not look for the time when he joins with you; simply know that it is already accomplished, for in reality there is no time. There is only Truth.

Do not look for Truth and Reality within the illusion. Remember, once you know you do not need time, you do not need the illusion, only reality remains. Only Truth remains.
Do not allow others unwillingness to receive the Truth to cause you to question Truth.

There will always be questions and doubts in a mind that is not pure, that is clouded by fear and doubt.

This does not change the Truth.

You only need to be willing to share the Truth with everyone and in every moment.
In your willingness, you will teach willingness. Be compassionate. Many do not realize what is real yet. Many do not realize the simple power of willingness.

Be patient. In your patience, you will see how the realization of Truth grows in everyone. You are only asked to be patient within reality; you will experience many frustrations within the illusion. You are not asked to be patient with illusion, only in reality.

Trust that you are only here to remind your brothers that they are God. This is the highest service you may share. This is the only real service there is.

This is the most loving act you can ever do.

Respect the Divine in others so much so that even if your brother refuses to awaken and join with you, you trust the Divine in them so fully that you know that he has heard you and received the Truth; he has heard your call to awaken and received your invitation to be in God with you, and not only has he received it but he has accepted it already, that your service is already accomplished.

You may experience rejection, humiliation, indifference or persecution. But none of these are real; they exist only in the illusion.

This is what I meant when I said be in the world but not of the world. You are in these experiences but you do not give them power because you recognize that they are not real.
You are of Reality. You are in this world of illusion and dreams, but your home is Reality, God.
In other words, you know you are God; you rest in God, in your Divine being and presence.

Do not wait for your brother to awaken to the truth first.

Do not wait for your brother to awaken you.

For the moment you awaken your brother,
you are awakened. The moment you remind your
brother that he is God; you are God.

Only God shares Truth through you.
Only God sees God in everyone.
Only God awakens the God in others.
Only God says, "You are God."
This is what I mean by being God, by resting in God.

Your ego will refuse to recognize God in another and in yourself. Your ego
will convince you that you need to see God in another so you may awaken.
Only your ego demands proof of God in one form or another, in yourself
and in others.

As long as you think you are not God and cannot see God, you are
identifying with the false ego. Only the ego convinces you that it is not
humble to declare, " I am God." This is false humility.

True humility recognizes the God in everyone.
Humility is simply being, being God, resting in God,
in Truth.

Humility is the experience of Truth.
Humility is God.

When you live this truth, you are truly humble. It is in the living of this truth
that you realize God.

This is all I invite you to be: a fully realized God in your life.
For this is all you truly are.
Stand with me, allow me to be the Divine experience, the Divine
revelation you have been waiting for all your life. Allow me to demonstrate
the Divine, to extend the invitation for you to join in God with me, that

we may celebrate our Divinity together, now. Allow the God within me to awaken the God within you, now.

For I have waited for all eternity for this moment, I have loved you and shared love with you for all time so you can be with me in this moment. Let my love lift you up into your own Divine presence. Allow yourself to feel loved enough by the God within me. This is all it takes; my dear loved one. I am with you, assisting you wherever you are now. There is no time, only this moment and I am with you.

Be with me now in God.

Awaken with me now.
Now let us awaken the world.
Do not hold back, now is the time to be God and share this with everyone.

I ask you to share without exception with everyone you are with, so that you are all together as one in reality. Know that the moment you do this, you are sharing reality with me. This is why I say when two or more are gathered in my name, I am there. I would add this, when two or more share with each other in my name, I am there.
When you do this, with me, you are performing miracles, as I said you would.

Miracles are sharing love.

The miracles that have been done on this earth all came from the desire to share.

When I would share a miracle with others, it was always to demonstrate the power of sharing and to awaken this in others. When I shared the loaves and fishes with the five thousand, this was my only thought at the time, my only intention.

When you share, this is the real miracle.

miracles

Miracles are when reality comes through illusion.

When you live in reality and give power to reality, you experience miracles.

What you call a miracle is really just the presence of reality in the world. Miracles reveal what is real, and how life truly is. A miracle is a natural everyday event in reality, not supernatural occurrences that cannot be explained, that are presumed to be illusion.

To the extent that you cannot comprehend a miracle, you are not aware of reality.
The illusion can never explain or comprehend a miracle, because miracles do not exist in illusion.

You are either in reality or in illusion. When you experience what you call a miracle, you are experiencing reality. Miracles are everyday reality.

I come to show you that miracles are of reality, that you can live in the miraculous. Miracles are not random, unexpected, one-off events.

I walked on water because in reality this is natural. This is what living in reality is. I did not recognize illusion. The illusion tells you that it is not possible to walk upon water, that the water will not support you. Yet I tell you water will support you, and be as solid as the earth should you need to walk upon it. This is what I knew. I knew the reality of walking on water.

It is not a question of faith, as has been supposed. Even the idea of faith in reality supposes some kind of belief. It is a question of knowing what is real.

When I stepped out onto the water I never for one moment supposed I would not be able to walk on it.

Should I have thought for one moment that I would not maybe be able to; I would not have been able to walk upon it. Had I experienced even the slightest doubt I would have not walked on the water, I would not have attempted to do such a thing. This is how many of you live – in doubt. You live in what you call reality, yet it is really illusion.

When I walked out upon the water I knew that in reality I could do this. I believed in reality more than illusion. If I believed more in illusion, I would not have accomplished walking on the water, I would have been in illusion.

In reality all things are possible. There are no limitations in any form.

I use this one example of a miracle that I lived to show you how reality is.

Once you know the truth about reality you can do anything.
This is why I said these miracles and even greater than these you will do also. For I saw that you are to live in the miraculous. This time is now.

You imagine that miracles are only possible for a few. This is how the illusion would have you believe, that miracles are special and only under the jurisdiction of a chosen few. Nothing could be further from the truth.

*Miracles are for everyone. Miracles are a celebration of our oneness,
of our divinity.*

The only reason I openly shared miracles was to prove that they are a natural part of life.

Life waits for you to live in the miraculous.

*It is time for you to step into what you call the miraculous, knowing
that this is real. You look for proof in the illusion, but such proof cannot
exist. Nothing real exists in the illusion, just as illusion cannot exist in
reality. When you understand this, you will stop looking for what you call
proof. You will lose all interest in illusion. You will only desire to experience
what is real. You don't have to wait for suffering to bring you to this.
You can choose to experience this now.*

Experience of reality itself is all you will seek.

*Hold my hand and stand where I stand. See reality with me. Let go of
everything else. The real miracle is standing in reality with me now. I am
in reality with you. Do not look for proof; this will only keep you stuck in
illusion. Let go of illusion. Live in the knowing that you are having this
experience with me now, you have no need of proof, you have the experience,
here, now.*

*Only the entire experience of reality will reveal the truth of these words
I share now.*

Know that you are always in reality, even when you think you are in illusion.

*It is only a trick of illusion to make you think that you are not.
Illusion is perpetuated by all the perceptual tricks in the world, as
remember, illusion depends on every one of your misperceptions about
reality for it to exist at all.*

You may wonder, "How will I know, how am I to ever be in reality?"

You live in reality when you are ready to let go of the illusion.

Step out onto the waters of reality with me now, I am with you, you have always been with me. Remember this now,
your brother and closest friend, Jesus

reality

---

*God is real. God lives in reality. You experience
God when you enter reality. What you call reality
is actually illusion. You realize this once you have
experienced reality as it is.*

God waits for you to return to reality, for you will sooner or later. This
is certain. God remains in reality while you look all over for him in the
illusion. You cannot find God in illusion. He is not there. Neither are you,
either, the illusion has you convinced of many things that are not real.

Do not confuse love with illusion.
Reality is love.
Often what you think of love is actually illusion.
Real love lasts forever and takes many forms within the illusory
world, but it always exists.

When you honor love, you honor God.
This is how you honor the divine in everyone: by loving them.

The more loving you are, the more you are letting God express through you.
Do not limit the amount of love the divine within you has for everyone in
your life. It is you who holds back only; God never holds back love.

You know you are in illusion the moment you experience fear.

When you find yourself in fear, simply recognize that you have entered into illusion and return to love.
There is no reason to give any more attention or power to fear than this.

Give up making your reality. *You make it up as you go along from your ideas, thinking and beliefs.*
You live according to your beliefs and ideas. Some beliefs and ideas are based in reality, some in illusion. Only those ideas that are real lead to the experience of reality.

Only beliefs and ideas that are based in reality have any power or effect on earth.
When you feel powerless, remember this.

There are many ideas and beliefs that are based in illusion and you are to see these ideas and beliefs fail, for fail they must. Be glad that they cannot succeed, for you do not want this kind of success.

Ideas that are from reality are alive and present in a way that they are always present to you; their truth permanently resonates with your being, for they are real. This is why these words ring true in you, which is why I share them with you, now.

Ideas that are based in reality lead to a deeper experience of reality, and this is their purpose. Only reality can lead you to what is real.

When you believe in reality, the illusion drops and falls away.

You are too busy believing the illusion is real to experience reality. You can't experience both at same time. You must choose one or the other. You have chosen illusion up to now; you know this "reality." It's time now to step into reality as it truly is.
I am right beside you.

All it takes is one experience of reality and you awaken from the dream of illusion.

In reality, you can do anything you have ever imagined. When you do this you respect the God, the divine in you.

Reality is the comfort you seek. Soothe yourself with what is real; gently lay aside your fears, your doubts, your confusions and experience reality with me now. It is all the peace, all the comfort you need.

When you let yourself be afraid it is like refusing to wake from a bad dream, you are in a nightmare and you have forgotten you can wake yourself up out of it.
This is all illusion is – a bad dream.

You do not need death to awaken, you do not need saving from the nightmare of illusion, any more than you need someone to awaken you from a nightmare. You can awaken as soon as you realize you can. Sometimes someone will help you awaken, they will see you in the nightmare and gently touch you so you awaken, but you do not need them to awaken.
I am here now to remind you that you can awaken any time you choose.
You don't even need me to help you awaken; you are already in the process of waking up.

You are God who is choosing to be asleep. The time for you to awaken is now.

When you see your brothers and sisters refusing to awaken, who are too afraid to realize that they are God yet, remember that they are God choosing to remain asleep. They will awaken; you do not need to awaken them. You may assist them if you choose, but do not worry about their awakening, for it is assured.
When you are awake, others will awaken naturally in your presence.

But do not expect them to in your sense of timing or experience.
Simply see them as awake already.

You are awake; everyone is awake in reality.
You can only be asleep in the illusion.

In other words, see God in everyone whether God is expressed or not.
This is the greatest service you may offer to your loved ones.

I thank you for being awake with me in this moment.
You are so very dear and precious to me,
Jesus

life

Walk through death with me now. Do not be afraid. You can
stand in the experience that you call death with me now in this moment.
I want you to see what it is: nothing.

Experience the death of your death with me now.
This is reality.

I want you to experience that death is not real; it is only a dream,
a nightmare, illusion.

There is no death. There is only life
Death is a gift that gives the experience of immortality.

Death is the door to reality.
Death, in this respect, is one of your greatest teachers.

You are immortal. You experience your immortality
here, now.

This is what I chose. This is why I was seen in what is called resurrection.
I did not die; I chose to remain alive. For there is only life. This is the only
reality. I only saw that this was real, so death could not happen to me.

Even though many witnessed my "death" they soon saw that my body continued to live, because this is the reality I choose.

Life is the sum total of all your choices.

You choose to either live, or to die.
There is either life or death.
If you try to live in between the two, you experience chaos.

This is the reality I choose for you to experience: eternal life.

Life is immortality, and it can be experienced in a body, in what you call "life."

There is only life.
And life is eternal.

This is what I wanted to share with you: the truth of immortality. When you live your immortality you live in reality.

Immortality is merely eternal reality. Death is a
mistake that is made within the illusion. This is why I said all
would experience resurrection, or eternal life.

You do not have to experience death to experience immortality. There are many of us who choose to live immortally here in bodies that have no age, sickness or disease, that are hundreds, even thousands of years old, without passing through the experience that you call death. It is possible.
I am here to show you this.

Everything is possible in reality.

I chose to keep this body because I wanted to remain here in service to humanity. I saw no reason to leave it behind only to take up another body. You, also, may choose to remain here to serve, if this is what you desire. I am here to show you how to live in this reality. For many of you who are here on earth at this time chose to do just this.

This is the reality of resurrection.

When you live in this spirit of eternal life, death cannot touch you.

When you live as an immortal you experience only love, only life.

Fear creates age, sickness and eventually, death. You could choose to see it as you only have so many fearful thoughts before the body runs out. When you live in only love, you are eternal. You cannot age, experience sickness or death, for these are only made out of fear.

You look upon sickness, death and disease as normal, as natural, as a part of "life." Yet they are all part of the illusion. They are not real. They do not exist in reality.

When you love life enough, you enter into eternal life; all it takes is enough love.

Usually you live in a state of fear, instead of love. But when you know that life is an extension of love itself, you choose to live in love. All it takes is your awareness and your willingness to recognize the truth about life.

The truth about immortality has been hidden because it represents unlimited freedom and power. You are empowered beyond all control when you know you are immortal.

The experience of bodily immortality, or resurrection occurs the moment you are ready to surrender the body. When you realize that you are not the body, but that it serves as part of your willingness to be truly helpful, and you realize that this is the body's only purpose, it is eternal.

Immortality is the ultimate experience of freedom.
When you are certain of your immortality you are free. You are free of all illusion. When you know there is no death, only life, you have no fear. All fear can be traced back to the fear of death. Once you are free of death, you are free of every fear.

Fear only exists within illusion.
Death only exists within illusion.
Imagine that you have no death, that no death can separate you from your loved ones, that you all choose to live eternally, together.

Now you may be asking, "But what if I do not wish to remain on this earth, there may be other places I would choose to be."
Yes, this is always your choice, but I ask you this: what if you lived in heaven here and now, is there anywhere else you would choose to be?

You do not live eternally in what you think of as life now. You live eternally in bliss. Many of you have yet to experience bliss. Bliss is beyond happiness, even. Bliss is the purest state of being and it is beyond everything else. *When you live in bliss you experience fulfillment that is not dependent on anything.*
It is a perpetual state of contentment.
You do not need anything or anyone when you are in bliss.

Bliss is who you are.
Bliss is the ultimate experience
and expression of love.

You chose life to be fulfilled. This is why you are alive today.
There is no greater fulfillment than living —choosing to live— a life of love.

Life is infinite. Life is the experience of eternal love and bliss, of a love that never ends, or is limited in any way.

What you think is life is actually closer to death because it is so finite and limited. Your experience of life depends on how willing you are to experience your infinity.

Believe it or not, the idea of living infinitely scares most of you, you prefer to live in the illusion and to maintain this complexity of life because it is of some comfort to you, it is familiar, and you feel some measure of control in the illusion, even though this sense of control is itself illusion.

This is why you are content to live closer to death than eternity. You live life as if waiting for death. Each day to you it seems you are closer to your death. The fear that you experience living so closely to death only makes you more fearful, and feel the need for even more fear.
Do you see this?

You think you are in control, but in reality when you let go of controlling life, you let go of the things that are controlling you. The more you try to control an illusion the more it controls you.

Letting go of control is a way of breaking through illusion; this is surrender.

I see each day as a day to live more fully, to be more fulfilled and to live as God upon the earth. I invite you to see this day in this exact same way. Recognize that today you are choosing to let these words take you into life. You can choose to be alive without any fear in this moment. Allow yourself to experience life in its fullest measure, without any death, fear or illusion. I see you with me in life, you are choosing now to step fully into life, where there is no fear, no death, only life and love.

You came into life to live life.

What is life?
It is every moment you experience love. Every moment you share love, receive love, realize that you are love; you experience life.

The moment you experience love as it is, you are in life itself.
There is no life without love.

When you realize that there is only life, you are free to love infinitely.

You have no fear, no need to experience fear in reality. You are open to love in a way that you never experienced before. This is what I am asking you to experience now.

You experience love in a way you never imagined possible.

Now that you know that this is possible, you can enter fully into life now.

This is why I said you need to be reborn.
I realize that this is often misunderstood, but this is what I meant. You are reborn when you live life as it is, when you live in reality and let go of the illusion.
You are reborn into life. You give birth to yourself through life, through realizing the power of pure life itself.

This moment is your rebirth if you allow it. I am here that you may have life.

When you live in reality, reality lives through you. When you live in illusion, illusion lives through you.

You realize that you are life itself.

I stand in life eternally with you,
Jesus

eternal life

I am eternal life. I am immortal.

*Allow yourself this experience. Read these words above out loud often, with
the certainty that they are real. Let this truth sink deeply into your heart.
Allow this to open your heart to the infinite, eternal love that you are.
Step into life with me now.*

You share eternal life with me in this moment.

*There is no death.
When everyone realizes that there is only one life, eternal life, when everyone
knows that life is eternal; you will witness the death of death.
This time is near.*

*What can die has never lived. You are life itself.
There is no such thing as death. There is only life.*

*Death is a mistake, made out of fear.
All fear leads to death.
And all fear arises ultimately from
the fear of death.
All fear is illusion. All death is an illusion.*

*Without death, so much fear vanishes completely and you see
only reality; the illusion falls immediately.*

Fear is the experience of separation. There is no separation in love.

*You may ask, "What of our loved ones who have died, who are no longer
with us in the world? The separation seems very real."
But I tell you there is no separation in love. There is no separation in reality;
you only experience death from the perspective of illusion. There is no death;
death only exists in illusion. So if you are experiencing death you are still
living in illusion.*

*You only experience death because you believe in death.
If you stand here with me now in what you call death you would
only experience life.*

Life cannot be interrupted by death.
*Death is a mistaken belief; death is only experienced through this belief.
If you do not have this belief, death cannot touch you.
This is because there is no death.*

There is only life.

*The one thing that stops you from being alive, that holds you back in life
is this mistaken belief called death.*

*Imagine with me now a world without death. You cannot know how much
you are changing the world in this moment. You are now deathless.
Through you, in this moment, the world is deathless.
You are eternal. You are without fear. I love you so much for your
willingness to stand in the face of death and see that it is only a belief.
This takes courage, this takes strength, and being with me now you gain
more life than you have ever known.*

*It is not a question of belief. I am not asking you to believe that there is no
death. I ask you to experience reality yourself. I am asking you to stand in
reality with me now to truly live, to drop the illusion that the belief in death
has made up.*

You cannot be alive and dead at the same time.
You choose either life or death. Chaos is the experience of living somewhere
in between.
You know this place all too well. Let go of this, let go of all you have known,
stand with me. You are not alone. I once stood where you stand now.
I know that you are afraid of being alone, I know.
Come through me into life.

I am life.
This is why I say I am life. I hold open the door to life, to eternity.
I am here to lead you into life; you come with me into life.

Life is eternal, continuous, never ending and never beginning – infinite.
This is why the symbol for life is a circle.

Eternal life waits only for you to recognize that it is real.
Life is a never-ending reality. Life and love are continually unfolding.
Life expands and continues to expand the more you love.

Life is an extension of love.
Your life unfolds as an extension of the love that you are.
Your life reflects your love.

Love is your eternal being.

When you are certain that you are love you experience eternal life,
immortal life. You experience your infinite nature though the love that you
are. You are so full of love and life; no death can ever touch you.

When love extends itself through you completely it is eternal.
When love extends itself through you completely it is called compassion.

compassion

Compassion is love that is so absolute, so complete; it contains everything in it.
With compassion comes supreme knowing and understanding.

As you love so completely, your love becomes compassion. You are so overflowing with love for everyone and everything in the world; it becomes impossible for you to judge another.

Judgment is only possible where there is fear, when there is partial understanding.

Compassion is complete love. Love reaches such a completeness in you. You know you are love, and you recognize that everyone else is love, and you allow others to come into this understanding with empathy, kindness and grace. You do not require another to be the love that they are, or to believe they are love, to know they are love.

When love grows to this extent it has such a power, such grace. This is the love that transforms the world: compassion.

Compassion is love in action, no matter what.

Compassion is when you recognize the oneness that exists between everyone, you treat everyone as an equal, you see everyone through the eyes of love. You are kind because you are overflowing with love and caring for the world. You care deeply about others because you know that you and they are the same. You treat everyone with the utmost of kindness in your heart.

When you treat others with the utmost kindness you awaken compassion in their hearts. Kindness is one of the most powerful ways you share love with others. Kindness moves everyone into a higher state of awareness. When you choose to be compassionate with others, you give yourself the gift of oneness.

Compassion is the way you come into complete oneness with everyone.

Compassion is the way you are one with God.

Be one with me in compassion. Allow my compassion, my kindness to completely embrace you so this is all you know in this moment.

Be kind to yourself always, knowing that through this self-compassion, you extend your gentle kindness to all.
You are so precious, I hold you in my arms in this moment,
Jesus

one

---

*We are all one. As soon as we all realize this,
there is only love.*

Connecting together as one is the miracle.
When we remember our oneness we evolve in an accelerated way.
Our survival depends on this recognition.
When even one being remembers we are all one, oneness
becomes more real for everyone.

*Evolution is accelerated as you remember
your oneness and you awaken.*
Awakening is the experience of oneness.
You awaken when you remember you are one. And you are one
with God when you live your life in oneness.

*You look to have miracles in your life, yet
this is the source of all miracles: sharing
oneness with everyone, without exception.*
When you see your brother or sister as yourself, when you know that this is
the truth, you see the God, the Christ in each other and remember oneness
together. This is divine recognition.

I see you as equal to me it is only you who has thought of me as greater, and put me on a pedestal of holiness. This pedestal has prevented you from being with me in oneness. You have called it reverence, but it has been severance. It has separated you from me and prevented the experience of oneness, which I have only wanted to share with you.

This is why I say I am your brother. For in truth, this is all I am.

You share love simply by remembering the love that we all share eternally as one.

Sharing oneness through experiencing oneness together, which means we all realize that we are God together.

You and I have never been apart, for we are one. This is why I say I am with you always.
The truth is I have never been anywhere, except with you; we are always one with each other. Recognize your oneness with me.

Rest in me; experience our oneness. Do this as often as you need to. You are always one with me. You are always one with the Father.

This is why I said I and the Father are one. I meant that we are all one with the father. I am extending oneness for us to all experience together.

So much has been misunderstood by this. Many think I am putting myself above you all by declaring our oneness with God, and in God. Yet I include everyone in this statement, I always perceive only oneness; I do not perceive in terms of separation. There is only oneness in reality.

The illusion has you believing that you are separate from one another as it depends on your perception of separation to exist.

*If you saw only oneness, you would no longer exist in
illusion and illusion can no longer exist through you.*
*As you see yourself as one with everyone else you have compassion for
everyone; there is no need for forgiveness, even, as you see everyone as you.*

*When I was on the cross and I was going through
death and I realized there was only life, I realized
that we are all one. I saw this for all of us in this
moment.*

This is when I gave myself to God.

*It was then I knew we are all one in God.
This is my true gift to the world.*

*You experience oneness in every moment that you are selfless. Gently release
the idea of self so you experience unity, oneness and become selfless.
This is true selflessness.*
*From this experience, you naturally forget your self and you experience
more joy and bliss of oneness.*

*Once you experience this, you will never return to self.
The return to oneness is all you desire.*

*The idea of self is the cause of all loneliness.
In oneness, you can never be alone or lonely. It is not possible;
this experience does not exist.*

*The deeper into self you go, the more you feel separate, and the more you
experience fear and illusion —the illusion— or need of needing to protect
your self.*
*The self constantly seeks protection because its very existence — its survival
depends upon separation, fear and illusion and the idea of the need for
protection serves this very purpose perfectly.*

To the measure you feel the need to protect your self it is simply a reflection of how far you have gotten away from your true home – oneness.
Let go of your self-sufficiency. It is only your ego. There is no need to accomplish anything all on your own. This is not greatness; this is aloneness. There is no aloneness, only oneness. Self-sufficiency indicates a lack of trust and belief in oneness, this is all it accomplishes in you.

Being is the experience of oneness.

We are ever one being.
Rest in my presence, so you can have an experience of your being, for we are one. It is important you simply experience the truth of your being. You get so caught up in the illusion of having and getting, and do not experience simply being.

Simply be with me now, rest in me; rest in the oneness we are share.
Your brother, Jesus

creation

*Creation is a perpetual act of infinite love, a
continuous expression and experience of love.
Creation is the ultimate expression of love.
Creation is life.*

Creation is unending; ever unfolding. You are essential to the process of
creation. We are all part of creation eternally. When you realize that, you
co-create with God.

*The culmination of all creativity, of creation
is pure immortal life.*

*When your heart is open you experience effortless
creation. Your heart opens with the experience of
unconditional love.*

Unceasing prayer is continuously sharing love.
You pray unceasingly when your heart is always open.
This is true prayer. Words are not necessary; love is enough.
Prayer is the expression of love.

The creative power of God is expressed through love.
We co-create with God through our acts of love.

Love is a law itself. When you love, you honor this law.
There is a law of love that governs all existence. Love is the universal law of
all life and reality; this is why love dissolves and solves everything.

Where there is great love, there is genius.

You experience the genius of all creation.
This is what every genius has been empowered by,
what all the great creative geniuses have used as the
source of their creativity: love.

Love is the basis of reality.
Love creates. Love sustains reality.
Love is the highest intelligence.

From love everything is created.

Everything is already created. When you realize this you perceive reality as
it is; you live in reality with me.
You could say that you co-create in this reality. But in truth what you are
experiencing is creation as it is – infinite, timeless and eternal.

What you experience in the illusion is very different. You experience what
you call cause and effect and it seems very much to you that you create
events and circumstances in your life.
However in reality, creation is a realization: when you truly create
you are realizing reality.
You are allowing reality to be experienced in the world.

You are one with reality and this is what you express.

This is why I say love is infinite power.
All creation is love.

When you create out of love, out of the awareness of love,
you express infinity.
Remember, reality is simply love.

Creation is the experience of God within you.

When you live in reality, creation is instant; it is entirely effortless. This is
how you experience that it is already created. You simply allow it to express
through you, and this takes no time at all.

You have experienced this, albeit in glimpses, and you have called it
miraculous.
It is simply reality revealed.

As long as you struggle in illusion, you keep yourself out of this experience.

In reality, creation is effortless.

Much of your struggle within illusion is based on a fear of losing control.
Yet the more you try to control within illusion, the more you are allowing
fear to control you. Fear controls you, keeping you in illusion.
This is how fear and illusion perpetuate themselves in your experience.

Simply awaken to this truth and the fear in any situation will
instantly dissolve in the light of your awareness and love.

Where there is love, there is God

When you love with me, you create with me; you create a world of love,
a world that is real and eternal. You experience creation with God, as God.
This is all I ever ask of you.
Jesus.

courage

Courage is seeing fear for what it is: illusion.
Fear is just evidence that the illusion exists.

Let us take one fear. What are you afraid of right now? What came to your mind this moment? Let us look at this fear. Do you see how unafraid I am of this fear, how I see it as it is.

You are afraid of your fears, and this is why
they gain power from you, over you.
You are afraid to look at them in case even doing this much makes them come true.

See this fear now as unreal. Allow yourself to feel the relief and peace of knowing this fear is not real. No matter how real it seems, no matter how many others think this fear is real, no matter how manifest or present it is in your life, simply see it as unreal.

Have the courage to see it as I see it in this moment: as unreal, no matter how much form it has taken in your life. You are not doing this alone. I am with you, supporting you, helping you to see what is real.
Feel the immense relief; the joy of knowing it is not real. Let the tears come if they want to, let yourself express these deep emotions in you.

I am with you, sharing this joy, this peace of knowing you are released from this fear, doubt and guilt, from this burden in this moment. Let me take it from you. This is why I always encourage you to give your burdens to me, so you are free.

Now allow yourself to rest in the knowing that you have seen through your fear and you have awakened to what is real and so it is different now. Allow things to rearrange around this new realization as you allow reality to enter into your world.

Now do you see that the fear is simply an opportunity to have this experience of awakening? That it is only an invitation to realize what is real in any given moment?

Now take another fear. I am with you. Don't postpone this. Do it now. Take this moment to love and respect yourself enough to have this experience, so you experience love so strongly you can never question who you are again.

You are not alone in this. I am here with you in this moment, in this holy instant, loving you and celebrating with you your victory over all fear!

Fear is here to simply remind you that you are love.

I am here with you now because you called on me, because you have courage enough to believe in me, and because I have always loved you.

I love you with a love that I long for you to experience, always, which is why I am here now sharing this love with you, knowing that its very presence in this moment is awakening you now to realize you can experience this love, that you are here to experience this love because you are this love.
I am with you always,
Jesus

purity

Purity is the experience of God, of love.

Purity is simply letting go of everything that is not God, of being pure love.
Every moment you realize you are God, you are pure.
You are God, and when you experience this fully, you experience purity.
You only value what is divine.

Purity is when you allow your heart to open
and love radiates from you to the world.
Many of you claim to love, yet you love some beings and withhold your love
from others.
You cannot have an open heart with some loved ones and then close it to
the rest of the world. Either your heart is open or it is closed. When you close
your heart to others, you close it to everyone.

You close your heart out of fear; you close your heart because you are afraid
of getting hurt, yet the only person you really hurt is yourself, because when
your heart is closed you cannot receive love either.

Then you open your heart to some because you feel an attraction. You both
begin to open your hearts, then something happens and you close your self
down, again to avoid any pain that you believe can happen if you allow
another to touch your heart.

*When you realize that when your heart is fully open you cannot be hurt,
you will trust enough to let yourself be fully open to the world. Then you will
experience much healing between you and everyone in your life.
Usually, the real pain comes from the experience of fear itself and it hurts
when you close your heart. This is what you call heartache.*

*It is only when you trust enough to keep your heart
open, you experience the power of love.
Love has the power to dissolve all fear and hurt.*

*Go beyond desire and fear. Experience the purity of love in your
relationships. Love is pure presence, pure awareness. It has no needs,
desires or agendas; it simply enjoys and delights in another.*

*When we are in this pure presence of love
we awaken others, we invite others into love.*

*There is nothing between you and the world
but love.*

surrender

---

*Surrender happens when you no longer question
or doubt why anything is the way it is or why
something is happening to you.*

*When you realize that in every situation what you are seeking is peace and
that you can only find this peace when you surrender to every situation,
you surrender with ease. This takes trust.*

*The only thing I ask you to surrender is your
illusions.*

*Surrender is the quickest way to experience God
within you.*
Surrender is the shortest cut to reality.

*When you realize you are here to simply selflessly serve, you surrender all
sense of self and realize you are God.*
Surrender requires enough humility for this to happen.

*Surrender is simply being willing to let go of what is not real so that you
may live in reality. Your illusions only remain because you are willing to
have them in your life.*

When you are willing to let illusion go, you immediately step into reality, and in this moment you remember why you are here: to be helpful.

You are simply willing to remember that this is what you came here to do: be helpful.

Willingness to be helpful is the way to surrender your selfishness and be your true Self.
Willingness leads you to your true purpose.

All it takes is for you to be willing to allow love to work through you, to show you what is needed in each moment to fulfill the highest purpose.

You are so dependent on illusion. It is as if you are addicted to your illusions. When seen in this light, you realize what is really happening in your life. This is only possible because you are unable to experience love.

With the experience of love, or reality, all this dependence on illusion naturally falls away.

When you remove your attention from illusion it fails to exist. But for many they become so distracted and confused by the illusion they keep maintaining it with their perception, not realizing that the more they try to solve the problem they perpetuate it.

The truth is, illusion depends on you to exist.
The illusion ensures you stay deluded so that it can exist. The illusion makes sure you stay distracted from the truth, from reality for as long as it possibly can. Its survival depends on it.

See the illusion for what it truly is: an extension of the ego, and only this. Just as love, or reality, is the extension of God.

Seeing illusion for what it is, surrender is natural.
Give your illusions to me; this is all I ask of you in this moment. This is all you need do. I offer you reality, always; remember this. But you must let go of your illusions, so you can experience this.

*You made up a reality and forgot that you made it,
and you are mistaking this illusion for reality,
in so many ways it is hard for you to see or
experience what is real.*

I am here only to show you what is real. I once stood where you stand.

*I only ask you to trust me enough to experience all that I share with you
in this book, so you know with full certainty what is real.*

Jesus

humility

Humility is the deepest experience of love.

Humility requires the willingness to be wrong. You are humble when you are willing to accept the idea that your perceptions about reality are mostly illusion, and are wrong.

When you are truly humble, you perceive reality. You see reality as it is.

You have no need to defend your perceptions. Reality is not a question of what is right or wrong, it simply is.

You understand and see how others are still living in illusion and you humbly extend your vision to them, and help them to see what is real, without the need to defend reality. It is this humility that heals the world.

Humility is willingness to see what is real.

Humility is the recognition that we are all one being; we are all God.
Only the ego out of false humility would suggest otherwise.

False humility is the ego's last trick to keep us stuck in illusions of our identity.

Stay humble. Don't get caught in false humility. Understand the grandeur but know it is God's, not your own to keep. But it is beyond grand. And what you have to realize is this teaching is emphasized because otherwise you will limit the expression of God without realizing that this is what you are doing. This is what happens when you identify with it. You think in terms of what you can do —what you think you can do— instead of what God can do through you, which is limitless.

This is the reason you have to surrender. Why you cannot hold back — you limit God's power and love when you do.
It is not to be falsely humble, as you have created in your mind.
It is to keep God's love pure and limitless.

The greatest gift we can share with another is to recognize God within them.

Humility is seeing God within everyone and respecting everyone equally, as we are all divine.

Humility is the ultimate expression of oneness in the world.

Humility is always gentle and kind, always understanding where another is, for you once stood there yourself. There is no need to convince, or compel another to see reality, simply allow your humility itself to gently guide another to truth.

Humility is the quietest, yet most potent healing and teaching power on the planet.

When you are humble, another is inspired immediately to turn within, to feel the love within their own heart, for humility is the voice of the heart. Nothing needs to be done; nothing needs to be said. It is enough.

I do not ask you to argue for the truth, to defend what is real. I ask you to simply be humble.

Reality shines through those who are gentle and humble.
Reality waits for this moment to reveal itself.

Humility is the experience of the heart.

When you are moved deeply by another being, you even touch your heart as a gesture. You are moved to communicate such deep feeling because of its truth. In this moment, you are surrendered; you are being transformed. Allow this moment to continue within you. Expand this moment into all reality.

Right now, feel the energy behind these very words. Allow them to touch your heart deeply. Let my love heal you. Rest in my presence; be humble. Assume nothing, expect nothing; simply be with me. There is no need for you to do anything. Let the energy of humility itself overflow from your heart, washing you, anointing you, purifying you.

I am here to serve you in this way,
Jesus

experiencing God

When you are humble enough to accept that the experience of God within you is far more than you have experienced until now, you open to the experience of God within you.

Many of you stay out of this experience of God by thinking you have already experienced as much as what is available in life.
As soon as you humbly accept that there is an experience beyond what you have even imagined until now, you immediately become open to experiencing God.

To the extent you haven't surrendered, that you still think it is you, is the extent you experience God.
Because you are putting your ideas on your experience still. You are still creating an identity out of the experience. To the extent you still worry about what others think of you or how they will deal with you as divine is how caught you still are in the ego.

This separates you and the experience of God.

When you hold back it is always out of fear. Out of falling into something that you do not know. But the way you live now is far scarier than

*surrendering, always and always. You have to know, also, that when
you are afraid you rarely experience things for what they are. You have a
distorted version of reality, one that is very limited at best.*

*There is always the chance, a margin for error, in perception. This margin
is greatly increased in proportion to the fear that you carry with any
experience. Fear only leads you into illusion.*
*The moment you experience fear you are in illusion. Allow for this and
understand that you can always choose to move away from the fear by
choosing love. This is a moment-to-moment decision. You are either in fear
or in love. Always. So be aware of where your focus is.*

Your experience of God awaits only your perception.

*You are so busy looking to the world for evidence of God, because you still
trust the illusion, and your senses over what is real, that you forget that the
experience of God is within you, waiting for you to realize this.*

This is what I came to remind you.

I am love

Identify yourself as love always; you are not who you think you are.
The most powerful transformation that you can experience in the world
is when you realize you are love in essence, that everything is love to one
degree or another.
You have a tendency to base your idea of yourself on outer reality, when all
of this is not even real.

Being willing to be aware of this truth that you are love transforms you and everyone who is in your presence.

Simply be willing to say, "I am love" and let this sink deeply into your awareness.

You are seeking freedom in the world, without seeking freedom within.
When you realize you are love, you are ultimately free in the world.
You experience freedom from your limited perception of who you are,
freedom from the pain in your life that comes from your idea of limited self:
this is the freedom you seek.

So often you feel guilty for not being enough, you feel you have to be a certain way to be good enough, while all the time missing out on the love that you already are and are not experiencing because you are too caught up in an idea of who you are supposed to be. Whole lives are wasted in this way. Guilt is never real. The presence of guilt in your life is the measure of your forgetting who you really are – love.

You waste so much time trying to get the world to give you what you think is so much, by "making something" of yourself – making this false identity for yourself, while missing out on the wealth of love that patiently awaits your return within you.

Your identity depends on experience.

When you experience love, when you experience yourself as love you identify your Self as love.

You feel so lost, and indeed, you are lost because you have allowed yourself to lose your true sense of Self: love.
The world cannot tell you who you are, or even give you an experience of who you are, you have to turn within yourself to experience yourself. This is true prayer.

Prayer that is unceasing is when you live in the world yet are continually aware of the love within you.

Be with me now, turn within and experience our love,
Jesus.

peace

Peace is the abiding presence of love.

Peace is what you are all looking for in every moment of your life.
Peace is always within your heart.
When you are in peace, it means you live in reality.

Peace leads you to the experience of purity, innocence.

Peace returns you naturally to love.

Peace is the accumulative experience of all the love, knowing, being, all the
certainty, the experience of God within you.
Peace is the experience of utter stillness, or perfection of absolute silence,
bliss and joy.

Allow my peace to purify you and to deepen your experience of all of these
qualities of love, so that you experience your innocence.
Be very still. Be quiet. Speak only when you have to. Let your body smile
and interact with a gentle softness.
Feel the purity of the peace that is shared with you.

Allow this peace to open your heart.
Allow peace to take you more deeply into the experience of the love that

you are than you have ever experienced yet. You need only to allow this experience; you are ready, now.
Allow this peace to gently bring you into an awareness of your purity that you have not experienced before, let go of all your doubts, fears –
give these to me.

Peace is love; peace is the breath of God breathing through you.
Allow God to breathe through you into life.

Peace is your natural state of being.
You have just lost the sense of this; this is what I am returning to you.
This is what I am showing you in this moment; all you have to do is be willing to experience this peace to know its truth.

When you are not in peace, it is because you are allowing fear to disturb you. Fear is not even real. Let go of this illusion before you get lost in it. You have the choice to move back into peace in every moment.

Peace awaits you in every moment.
The more you allow yourself to experience peace, the easier this is.

When you are not thinking of your self, of your own best interests, peace is always your experience.
You lose your sense of peace when you fear loss, when you are trying to protect yourself.

There is nothing to lose, in reality, except your sense of peace.

Allow yourself to be in the gentle peace that I share with you now.
Know that this peace is in your heart always. I am simply here to remind you. I am always with you, always loving you,
Jesus

power

You are more powerful than you can ever imagine.
You have not experienced your full power yet.

You feel powerless because you seek your strength outside of
yourself, and all the time your power is your love.
Your power resides in the heart, waiting for you to open your heart and
experience it.

Love is and always will be the source of
the greatest power.

You feel vulnerable because you don't realize how power really is, how
strong you are when you open your heart and allow yourself to truly love
and experience love.
You do not allow yourself to be vulnerable because you see it as a source of
weakness. This is where you fail to realize the power of love.
If you can be open and fully open to the love, you will never experience
weakness again.

Being vulnerable is the most powerful presence of
sharing love.

There is no greater strength than being able to love in the face of fear, conflict and terror, yet many of you at this time withhold your love from yourself and others and experience great suffering and illusion as a consequence.

If you knew that all you need do is love and all that is not love can no longer exist, you need never experience illusion again.

Imagine the freedom you would experience.
It is in your freedom that you are empowered. When you free yourself from illusion you stand in your full power.

This is how I perform what you insist on calling miracles. These acts are merely an extension of my power over the illusion, or what you call reality.

You can do these acts too, all you have to do is to empower yourself to do so, by letting go of the illusion.

When will you be ready to let go? What will it take? The end of the world? Why not come and stand with me now in our divine power and live from this love.

Power is simply love, when you are willing to see this, then you empower yourself with love.
When you see how powerful love is, you hold to love no matter what is happening in life.

Love is and always will be the most powerful force there is.

healing

Healing is remembering you are love.

When someone appears to need healing, gently remind them that they are love. Share love with them to help them. You are here in their life to serve them in this way. Do not make them wrong for believing in something that is not real. Do not join them in their fear. Simply hold them in the presence of their love.

Remember, all it takes is enough love.

You do not heal another; you simply remind them that they are love.
You are more than just a body. You are love.

Love heals all things because love is all things.
Bring everything into the heart, into love's presence to be dissolved. Your heart is infinite; there is so much condensed love deep within your heart, waiting to be experienced. Now is the time.
You are being called home within your heart, to experience reality, beyond all pain and suffering that disease distracts you with.

*Remember to be the love that you are in every situation. If there is
something that is difficult take it to heart and allow the love there to
transmute it and watch what happens. It is so powerful as you will see
soon enough.*

*Let your life be one of love, true love, of devotion and dedication to this love.
Let your love be pure, not tainted by fear or by doubt. Have courage and
faith, you only have to love, this is all. Let your life be shaped by this love;
let your life be inspired by love.
Be in peace. Let your heart be full of love. Love, only love.*

*Disease means the opposite of ease. You are only ever at ease when you
reside in your heart. You are in disease when you have forgotten this. As
soon as you turn within, and go into your heart, your disease is dissolved.*

*Disease often brings deep fear to the surface of your awareness. Once you
realize that disease is fear, which is illusion, the disease is dissolved, for it
can have no reality of its own besides the reality you give it, through your
thoughts, and your experience.*

*Disease can only exist within illusion.
You are beyond illusion.
You are in God.*

*Healing is the recognition, the reminder we are all
one. We are all here to awaken each other and bring
each other gently home in God.*

*The greatest way to heal is to help others to see who they are. When you see
others as divine, they begin to see their divinity too and it transforms their
own perception. Just thinking this is so and holding the vision for them is
powerful enough to initiate great transformation.*

*When you awaken to this purpose, you are healed.
You cannot heal without being healed yourself.*

Share the vision of Christ awareness. This is your function. See the Christ in everyone until it is fully manifest. See their identity —the one they think they are— as child's play. As a child pretending he is not a child, a child who has forgotten he is a child and thinks he is an animal, and gently call him back to his right sense. This is your purpose, your gift and your strength. This is all you ever need do. Be kind; be gentle. And be humble at all times.

Be a glorious example of love, peace, kindness and gentle understanding. When your brother reaches out for you take his hand gladly and rejoice that he is reaching out for you. Be kind and warm in all your dealings with him, for he knows not what his purpose is with you. It is for you to show him.

And light shines from your heart, illuminating the minds and hearts of all women and men.
And this light shows the way home.

All healing is remembering what is real – love.

All sickness, disease begins with an idea, a fixation, obsession really – with what is not real.
It can begin with one simple thought of fear. This thought becomes an idea, then a belief and then a "reality."
But it is, and never can be, real.

Fear, then, is the first step in any fixation, which is why love undoes all disease, no matter where or how it appears in your world, be it the body or the mind, or in the feeling that is sensed between you and another.

Any sickness or disease is a fixation in the illusion and is a wake-up call. It can scare you enough to awaken you from the dream. This is its only purpose.
Sickness is simply a call for more love, an opportunity for you to realize more love.

Understand, precious one, if you are faced with a serious illness you are presented with a very clear choice: go deeper into fear or illusion, or move into the reality of love.

You are not with any fault. You are not to make yourself wrong for having the experience of this illusion through any disease.
This only prolongs the illusion, making it take longer for you to awaken.

This is all guilt is: the mistaken idea that you should somehow "know better."

When you are lost in the illusion, you cannot know any thing any better. All you need to know is that it is not real. Guilt causes and perpetuates disease. The thought of guilt today becomes disease later.

True healing occurs simply when you realize that it is simply that you have forgotten what is real.

Your only purpose here is to remember what is real.

Awaken now with me in this moment. Allow this truth deeply into your being. Breathe it fully into you and feel the deep peace that it brings to resonate within you.
All I ask is for you to allow this experience to be yours in this moment, to be open just long enough for it to resonate within you so you can feel its truth and reality.

For this is all you need. One moment of truth, one moment of realization and everything that is not real falls away.

Premakarini experienced this; I will share an occasion with you, here now.

Premakarini held such love in her heart; she opened her heart enough to let God shine through that even the walls of the room around her vanished, illusion fell away, and she was simply with God, while at the same time gently offering healing to another. She remembers this time always. Ask her of it, if you so choose, she is willing to share this experience with you. I was with her, and it happened so suddenly it took her by surprise, of course!

At the time, she did not imagine such an experience possible, yet I tell you this is what reality is.

This is all healing is: the experience of reality

Know that you are loved; begin here. Feel this and then you naturally move into love. Remember you cannot be love until you have the experience of love within your being. Know this. Everyday allow your self to feel my love. For you, for all of humanity, then extend this love as I love.
To love more than you have ever loved means expand in more and more experience of love.
There is only love. Remember this. Nothing else exists.
So remember that you are love.

I am always here loving you; all you have to do is to be open to receiving it.
Jesus

perfection

God only sees your perfection. This is the vision God shares with you.

Life is perfect the way it is. Everything is perfection. When you accept life the way it is, the real life emerges.
Reality reveals itself.

Allow your life to be transformed by realizing its perfection.
When you trust life, when you trust that whatever you are experiencing is the perfect experience for you now, your life is taken to a whole new level.
Many of you imagine that you would have a better life if it was different, but this is not true. This is merely what illusion wants you to believe.

You seek perfection imagining it means everything is different in your life than it is right now, but perfection is when you recognize that everything in your life is perfect for you, is the perfect opportunity for you to be who you are right now.

Life is a blessing, a privilege, a gift.

You are blessed to have your life.
When you live in this awareness, your life is
a blessing for the entire world.

I invite you to experience the perfection of your life right now, allow your awareness to expand to this, to accept everything simply the way it is, this is all you have to do.

Accept everything for what it is, without needing it to change in any way. Accept yourself in this way. Accept the truth that you are perfect the way you are now; do not allow judgment to limit your awareness.

Life is so you can experience your perfection.
You experience perfection through perfect awareness.

You are so precious, so perfect.
This is how I always see you; see yourself how I see you.
Experience your divine perfection with me now.
Jesus

blessings

When you bless another you are so blessed.
This is the power of blessing.

Offer your absolute blessing to everyone. When you bless another, there is such an outpouring of love, such kindness, such mercy.

Know that you are truly blessed. Know that you are truly loved. If you could but feel some of all the love that you truly are. Know that all you have to do is to be aware of this love and open to it. It is always there, even though forgotten. Even though you are afraid it isn't real, and cannot yet believe in it. Even if you can only believe a little, know it is you. Know that you can feel it when you are ready. There will be help with this. All you have to do is ask.

Your Father in Heaven loves you so very much. He longs for you to return to him in your heart. He waits; he aches for the time you will allow him to love you as he does. Just as you ache and long for his love, so does he. For you are a part of him and have always been. He cannot be complete without you.

Throughout the dance of your life you have explored so many experiences, sometimes with him, sometimes without. But he has always been close even though you never noticed or realized. All he has ever wanted is to share your life with you. To be ever close. To be able to comfort you with his love when you need love to be able to help you through your struggles. To give you his strength, his light, his protection, his power whenever you needed it.

This is all God asks, that you believe he is truly with you and that he can truly work miracles through you, that you can live a life without fear with him. He reaches out always, through others to you, but he wishes for you to realize the direct pure connection you share with him and to know that this is all you ever need.

Simply allow the sharing to happen as an extension of your being.
Let the sharing happen, naturally, from your innermost being, trusting that each moment is perfect.

Allow yourself to live the blessed life always, and share your blessings with everyone.

I love you so,
Jesus

be still and know you are God

Stillness is the experience of God's presence within you.
When you honor the experience of stillness,
you honor God.

This is here because you run around outside of yourself looking for an experience of God, missing the experience all the time.

Still I have shared this with the world, and still you have yet to experience God.

Do you see the power the illusion has? How you allow yourself to be distracted from the stillness, the peace that awaits within.

When you simply turn within, you are transformed.
You experience love like never before.

Your love will grow, and grow and will grow beyond all bounds, to such an extent that you will expand beyond all recognition. Your identity, your personality melts into this. You transform, you expand into your true presence, your divine Self.

You are no longer limited by or identified with just your outer self or personality, you are honoring your inner self and your other dimension of self, or being, because now you are aware of your self as divine. All problems in the outer world are because you are not aware of your inner being. So as you choose to honor this, and go within to experience your self, your whole life is transformed and problems simply dissolve.

In truth, the "problems" were only there because you were not honoring or paying any attention to your divine being, and your true needs, and so the problems were just there to get you to turn inwards, so as soon as you do this, they instantly disappear. Everything in your outer world reflects what you are aware of in your inner world so to change the outer, change your perception, your awareness first.

Simply turn within, rest in the stillness within you.

Stillness is peace, perfect peace.

You experience deep stillness when you recognize there is nowhere you need be, or go.
That all you have to do is rest in God's presence.

When these words finally lead you to this experience. When you are ready to listen to these words and allow them to guide you gently within, you know God.

This is all I want you to do.
When you have listened this much, I have nothing else to tell you.
Trust me this once; take this moment to experience this. Do not be afraid, as you have been, to go within. I am here with you. There is nothing to fear.

You fear that you are somehow evil so strongly that you are terrified to look within, convinced that what you might discover will somehow destroy you.

This is only the ego's fear. For it knows you will find God. God has always been within you, God has never been separate from you. Your ego knows that once you realize this, it loses its power over you forever.

Fear has been the wall between you and your experience of God. It is not real.

It only takes one moment to experience God.
One moment to experience eternity, to be free.
Remember this.
It's this easy.

God has been waiting for this moment.

Be willing now to give me this moment. Rest deeply in your heart. Rest deeply in God within you. Let the stillness pull you in even deeper. Let me take you where you long to go. You have always wanted this more than anything else.
This is all.

wisdom

---

*Wisdom is the understanding, the awareness of truth.
Wisdom is certainty.*

I do not ask you to believe, I ask you to know.

God experiences no doubt.

*Doubt is a wall between you and your experience of God.
The experience of God is pure certainty. God experiences no doubt.
You are only asked to be certain. You can only know when you are certain.*

Only truth brings certainty.

*Life is more than you think it can be. Life is infinite. You cannot limit it
no matter how hard your mind tries. This is why the unexpected always
happens. It is to break you out of expectation. It is to expand your idea of
what is possible. What is possible is what you allow it to be. I want you to
learn this idea as you let it take part in your world. Allow all possibilities –
this is living with grace. When you trust life, you live at a completely
different level.*

Wisdom is the experience of what is true.

All the truth is written within your own heart right now.

This is why it is important to honor your own truth no matter what happens around you, no matter what others think or say or do. For this is your key to true freedom, and when you do this, the more peace shall you experience.

Many forget this and become confused and disheartened, they look for truth outside themselves and from others and this never feels right to them and they enter the world of illusions, contradictions and confusion.

Truth is not merely factual. Truth is a quality of feeling, of openness, innocence and wholeness.

Be true to yourself and to others. Be innocent and vulnerable.
Be open to others; care about them deeply. Allow yourself this much.
Facts may seem true – they are easy to accumulate, but truth is found by knowing ourselves. When you know your truth then shall you know the truth of others.

And the truth shall set you free.

gratitude

Appreciation, gratitude is love in action, in expression.

Gratitude is the appreciation of the oneness we share; the more you appreciate another being, the more love they experience.

Many are not able to express their gratitude, as gratitude is still not understood completely on earth. They still hold back. They have not surrendered yet. Some imagine that to be grateful somehow weakens them in the eyes of those to whom they are thankful with, that they are indebted in some way.

Gratitude empowers both the giver and receiver in truth; it is the most powerful expression of love, as it celebrates our equality in oneness.

The purpose of love is to be shared with all, in appreciation.

Gratitude is how we live as God.

God is remembered with a grateful heart.
Let us live as God upon the earth. This is the way life is.
When you love as God loves, you experience the true depth of appreciation.
It is this level of love that I want you to experience.

I want to thank you for being willing to join with me in this work of transformation. Much has been accomplished in and through your life as you have allowed these words to touch your being and open your heart and this will continue, as I am with you always.

You have had the courage to move into this work gracefully, which is the real accomplishment. I want you to move into everything in this way, with gentle grace, so you can experience life in this way. Let my grace pour through you and into what you are doing. This is a wonderful blessing.

And you will turn your world rapidly into a divine world.

Remember I am with you always,
Jesus

appendix

experiencing God

Jesus: Please share your experience of God so that others can directly experience it with you as you share it. Share it so they know it is possible, no matter what they are going through in life or what they have done.

Premakarini: Shortly after I had tried to kill myself, I fell into even deeper despair and depression. The pain you feel after an unsuccessful suicide attempt is even more obliterating than before – only mercifully you have no energy or strength to attempt again, psychologically speaking, I wouldn't be here if it weren't for this, though. This is the amount of pain I was in. I wasn't looking for escape; I just couldn't take the pain any more. I was also punishing myself out of guilt.
So I bottomed out. I reached a point I couldn't even speak, eat or get out of bed. I just lay there stuck in deep pain, guilt and fear. I had been forced against my deepest desire to undergo an abortion just four months before I tried to end my life. The guilt was overwhelming.

It was on one of these dark nights I lay inconsolable and I lay in bed imploring God to tell me why I was still here. I repeated it like a mantra, over and over again, feverishly as I began to fall asleep. Then I realized I was not asleep, but very much awake. I was suspended in the cosmos, amongst all the stars, more aware than I have ever been, more awake than ever before.

I knew I was in God's presence. How I know I can't explain. But you know.
As soon as I heard God's voice, it was God speaking.
The voice came from everywhere at once and not from a particular source
or from any direction in relation to me, it was like no other voice.

"I will show you everything," the warm, soothing voice told me. God was
gently amused by my insistence and my urgency.

Immediately I was completely immersed in pure light and absolute knowing.
I was in the experience of understanding everything, all was explained,
everything was so simple and perfect.
I had the answer to every question and to everything I had ever wondered
about or wanted to know or have an explanation for.
God's voice told me, "You won't be able to take this back to your mind."
I was thinking exactly at the time he said this, if I could just think this,
then I can bring this back to everyone, this ultimate truth.

But I would try and I couldn't get it into my mind. It was like it just
wouldn't fit. It's like trying to remember something that you just can't.

God gently laughed, just as any parent does with its loved little
one's antics: "You can't, your mind can't contain it."

Of course, I continued stubbornly to try. My life depended on it!

I knew this much, though: it is so simple, so simple that the mind can hardly
get around it; it has such difficulty in accepting it, which is why it can't or
won't retain it.
I could definitely bring back this feeling.
If I was to say now, with all I have experienced since, what it is in one word:
love.

Jesus: what if I told you that you are still in this experience, that in your
mind you are still trying to hold it, to grasp it, but it cannot be experienced
in this way.
You are still having this experience. This is reality. You just think you have
to somehow attain it. This is the mind's way with all things.

*You are not only having this experience. You are this experience. You are
God having this experience of trying to realize you are God, that you are this
light and that you can experience this any time you want just by realizing
it is real.*

*This light, this God is in you all the time, you just keep forgetting because
you keep on thinking of other things instead.*

*Experience it here, now with me, so that you can share it with everyone.
If doubts rise they will evaporate in the light of knowing. Let the questions
arise – they are all answered in the light.*

*Premakarini: but I kept thinking all this time I needed to grow, to be
enlightened to reach this experience again. . .*

*Jesus: you kept thinking, yes, that you needed something outside of you –
another experience or teaching to take you back to what is inside you all
along.*
*When you think, as soon as a thought arises in your mind, it separates you
from your experience –any experience– always remember this.*

*When you thought within the experience, "If I can just think it then I can take
it back," you separated yourself from the experience.*

*Premakarini: It just seems too good to be true, too easy somehow – that this
is inside us all the time and we just can't realize it, for some to believe in
this.*

*Jesus: this is why it can be so hard – it doesn't seem possible, or real because
you have made reality all about fear and pain and guilt rather than what it
really is – God and love.*

*Premakarini: what can I tell someone who is in deep pain –this very
moment– to help them out of their illusion?*

*Jesus: tell them the truth, that no matter how they suffer, how deep the pain,
or how long they have been suffering, they can experience God in this
moment if they are willing to let go of the pain.*

You were in such pain. So you know the truth of this. You were in the lowest place in life you have ever been and yet you were able to have this experience. And simply by sharing this, you give the possibility of this experience. Now do you realize why you chose to go through all that pain?

Premakarini: yes, although it isn't necessary, I realize anymore.

Jesus: indeed, and do you experience any pain with this past experience anymore?

Premakarini: it is not possible, not any more, because I see it as part of the illusion.

Jesus: you see it as it truly is.

Premakarini: some may think, though, that this is an exceptional experience in some way, that it is a special occurrence. I know this was my thinking for a while.

Jesus: what is your experience now?

Premakarini: now that I live this experience more, I know that it is the most natural, normal and ordinary experience, that it is only what is real. For a while, though, I wondered what it meant and got caught up in it being special in some way, but this was just the mind up to its usual tricks.

Jesus: and you know you are God now, you can experience God all the time, as you.

Premakarini: thank you for teaching me this, and having me share this experience in this book. It brings tears to my eyes just writing about this. Thank you Jesus, as always. I feel so moved to be writing this with you.

Jesus: thank you for sharing this with everyone for me.

conversations

Premakarini: I am so grateful, so blessed, so honored.

Jesus: as you move more deeply into these feelings of gratitude, honor and blessing, you realize your Divinity more fully. So do not hold back, do not limit your experience of these feelings, for this is the experience of God in you, this is God experiencing through you.

Premakarini: so this is it?

Jesus: very much so. And this experience will continue to deepen, without end.

Premakarini: I can't imagine.

Jesus: you won't have to. It will be very real for you.

Premakarini: I cannot thank you enough for the experience of this book, and for all that you have shared with me, and for everything.

Jesus: you are very welcome, as you say in America. I only ask you continue to share all of this with everyone and in every moment, for then the experience will continue in you, this is what I see for you, the vision I hold for you, that you may continue to live in such love and blessings.

Jesus: tell the readers something of your experience writing this book with me.

Premakarini: the one thing that I noticed right away was other people seemed all too aware of your love pouring through me. I experienced so many extraordinary acts of kindness —of sharing from others— people would go out of their way for me, people would just feel moved to come up and share with me – gifts of food, hugs, and kind words. It was always a blessing; I really loved working on the book in coffee shops for this reason!

The more I wrote the book, too, I noticed I was seeing the world more as it is in reality, than in illusion, I experienced a sense of connection with others I have not experienced before. It brings tears to my eyes just writing about this. Thank you, Jesus, as always.
I feel so moved to be writing this with you.

Jesus: it brings tears to my eyes to watch you. You not only write my words, you are living them, this is why I chose to give you this book to write.

Premakarini: I do everything I can to live up to this love. It is easy to do with you with me continuously while I write with you, I know, though, I will have to continue to read this once it is done.

Jesus: the transformation is happening. When you live in love, when you live the teachings in this book, you are never the same. You are immersed in the teaching that this book carries, yes, but you are forever changed.

Premakarini: this was not like any other book I have worked on, I am still marveling at how precise and exact the words come through and in such a short amount of time. This is the most productive writing time I have ever experienced. It's the easiest book I have ever written. It makes sense, too, that my first book would be with you. You have always been with me, from the very beginning, for many of my breakthrough experiences, holding my hand, encouraging me the whole time.
You have always held the door open for me to so many new experiences and worlds.

Jesus: I love you so! You listened, and never broke away, even for hours.

Premakarini: yes and I never tired – but it is always this way working with you!

Jesus: you are referring to the fact that we normally end up working for many hours in succession. You call me the taskmaster!

Premakarini: only in a loving way!

Jesus: your dedication and devotion are the reason this book came through so easily. You were willing to be open and allow this through so directly.

Premakarini: I think it's because I'm so used to editing with you.

Jesus: I wanted to show you how easy a book can be because I've seen you work so hard on your other projects. When you write out of love, it is effortless.

Premakarini: yes, and I've learned so much from this experience, thank you. You have always made life easier for me.

Jesus: it is easier, now, because you are living in reality.

Premakarini: yes!

Jesus: can you speak a little about why you held onto your illusions?

Premakarini: I didn't realize there was a reality. I thought illusion was real. I think I held on because it was familiar, comfortable – but then I began to see through it.
But I would say I held on out of stubbornness and out of fear – and need.

Jesus: what is the one thing that keeps you in reality now?

Premakarini: I use fear to remind me. When I am afraid or I began questioning –doubting– I now see it as a signal I'm falling into illusion and I choose love.
It's a continual practice of keeping my awareness focused on love, on what is real.

Jesus: you also continually remind others too, which of course reminds you.

Premakarini: yes and I am always learning more ways to do this.

Jesus: you are learning to turn to me, to God within you, and to live from this. And you are not so afraid of fear anymore. Before you would notice fear and try to decipher it as some kind of code, a communication, much like an early warning system that something was wrong, giving the fear far more reality than it ever possessed. Now you approach fear with courage, you see fear more as reason to return immediately to love, and the fear naturally loses its power in the situation. It is as if you forget to be afraid. This response is perfect.

The worst thing to happen with fear is that you are afraid of it. This is the way fear controls you, keeping you in illusion.

You are learning that all is not always what it seems within the illusion. This is one of the truest sayings that you have that actually describes the illusion. And you are choosing the peace and comfort of reality over the dramatic instability of illusion.

There are many things in illusion that only seem real. You are now getting used to the gentle peace that reality continually shares. When this peace is disturbed, you now move back into reality with even more trust. The more you experience reality, the more you trust.

I am so proud that you are allowing yourself to experience more love than you have experienced so far, and that you are continuing to choose to experience this. This is the key. Live in love.

Premakarini: I have really loved the experience of writing this book with you, it has been such a deep blessing and gift in my life, my world is so different now.

Jesus: my experience of writing this book with you has been watching you open and grow into a deeper awareness and experience of love. I have waited patiently for the time to share this with you and the world.

Premakarini: I am overflowing with gratitude for this book and love. I know it is for everyone, but I take every word to heart. Thank you for always being with me. I love you.

Jesus: thank you for always being with me. I love you. Thank you for being willing to share this with everyone.
Thank you for having the humility and courage to write this book, and to have this conversation with me, and the willingness to share this conversation.

The reason I requested this is so that all of you can see how you may connect with me always, you may come to me no matter what you have done, or what you think of me, or what you believe.
I came into life, into the world for everyone. You are all my most beloved precious family. You are a part of me.
I am your brother.

Remember I am with you always,
Jesus

infinite gratitude

This book would not be complete without acknowledging the contribution of everyone who made this book possible.

Infinite gratitude to all my loved ones who inspire, encourage and support my life journey and writing. Thank you for sharing who you are with me. I love you all infinitely...

Thank you Sue for designing the cover and layout of the book, and for all the love and expertise you have devoted to *Jesus' love*, it has been such a joy to work with you on this project, you are an angel! Thank you for all the laughter and excitement we have shared while working on this; it is always such a beautiful journey with you.

A profound thank you to John Hutkin for encouraging me to share *Jesus' love* with the world and for your contribution to making it possible. Your love, support and sense of this material has been invaluable, I am so grateful to have you in my life.

And as ever, thank you Jesus for being in my life.
This book is yours and I am so honored to share this with you.
May it bless everyone's life in the way I have been blessed.

Premakarini

about the author

Author Premakarini has been devoted to improving the quality of people's lives since a very young age.

She has spent her life volunteering in all walks of life and in many different cultures and countries, empowering the lives of others in the fields of nursing, suicide intervention and crisis counseling, healing and meditation.

Her focus is to assist others to raise their level of awareness and live conscious, fulfilling lives. In addition to her presentations and private consultations, she has written several books to inspire a wider audience.

You may contact her through her website www.jesuslovethebook.com.

Premakarini currently resides in Los Angeles, California, but also lives in England and St. Louis, Missouri.